VAUXHALL

A HISTORY

VAUXHALL
A HISTORY

ROBERT COOK

TEMPUS

First published 2005

Tempus Publishing Limited
The Mill, Brimscombe Port,
Stroud, Gloucestershire, GL5 2QG
www.tempus-publishing.com

© Robert Cook, 2005

British Library Cataloguing in Publication Data.
A catalogue record for this book is available from the British Library.

ISBN 0 7524 3416 0

Typesetting and origination by Tempus Publishing Limited
Printed in Great Britain

CONTENTS

ACKNOWLEDGEMENTS

In particular I would like to thank Vauxhall Motors without whose help and support this book would have been impossible. Vauxhall archivist Dennis Sherer was a guiding light from the outset, doing everything he could to help me with the project and always most hospitable. I am extremely grateful for the interest and support that Deborah Atkins, marketing manager of Vauxhall Heritage Services, has given to this project.

Thanks also to Dave Hinds and Andy Boddy in the Vauxhall Heritage Centre, not only for their help and but for allowing me to intrude upon their lunch breaks and for listening to my thoughts and observations on life in general whilst I enjoyed some excellent cups of tea, as well as being able to study their amazing collection of historic Vauxhalls. Further thanks to Frank Ford and Owen Hardisty for sharing some of their memories. The company has historic links with Australia and I am very grateful to my cousin, Sandra Condon, and her husband Pete in Victoria, for helping with research. Also in Australia, thanks are due to Les Coleman for sharing some of his memories.

I would also like to thank the many people who have talked to me about Vauxhall cars and Bedford Commercials and their experience of working, driving and owning them. I am also grateful to series editor Campbell McCutcheon, who shares my interest in Vauxhall and Bedford, for supporting this project. I am also indebted to so many writers and journalists, like Len Holden, who have written on this subject before me and thus informed my judgements. Thanks are due to the British School of Motoring, Freda Eastlake, Keith Oakley, Andrew Shouler and the Scilly Isles Steamship Co. Thanks also to Bernie Pardue, Barry Harvey, Keith Oakley and Dave Allen. Final thanks to my wife Nicola and to my mother for helping me to gather additional items relevant to this tale.

INTRODUCTION

Many motorists are aware of how awful British roads have become, of road rage, dangerous driving, and dreadful accidents. We have a history of penny-pinching governments, some wanting to milk the economy for taxes to pay for their bureaucracies and social projects. The last thing they want to do is invest in transport, preferring to blame middle lane motorway 'hoggers' for all the hold ups, chaos and carnage. Life has never been that good on our roads. In 1835, there were 3,300 stage coaches and 700 mail coaches, and accidents were many fold. This did not deter the human desire to break new ground. The travelling spirit is strong among the British and today's car has become a personal statement. Every year the nation's illustrious motoring origins are celebrated by a cavalcade of ancient cars on the London Brighton run. The February 1967 edition of *Vauxhall Motorist* commented on the experience of that year's run riding in to Brighton in the preserved 1904 Vauxhall: 'Our single piston speeded up and the catapulting motion smoothed out into a pleasant vibration.' No wonder motoring became so popular so quickly for those who could afford it!

St John C. Nixon informed readers of *Vauxhall Motorist* in February 1969 of a motor trial that had helped the British Motor Industry:

'At the early hour of 7 a.m. on Monday, 23 April 1900, there gathered at Grovesnor Place, Hyde Park Corner, London, no fewer than sixty-five motor vehicles of almost every description. They were to attempt what the great majority of the public considered impossible – a journey from Grosvenor Place to Whitehall.

'This was far the most strenuous trial of motor vehicles ever held in England... via Bristol, Birmingham, Manchester, Kendal, Carlisle, Edinburgh, Newcastle, Leeds, Sheffield, Nottingham and London... 1,000 miles.

'The trial was organised to (overcome)...prejudice about motor cars... to assist designers to decide whether to concentrate on petrol or steam, horizontal or vertical engines, pneumatic or solid tyres, water or air cooling, chain and shaft drive or belt drive, tiller or wheel steering, electric or tube ignition and other matters of the moment.'

Survivors of this epic journey were expected back after 2½ weeks, with speed restricted to 6½ miles per hour. Cars have since come much further in terms of safety, style and performance.

In just one month of 2004, 439,365 new cars joined the congestion on British roads. Motoring is more popular than ever as life on the road continues like a moving picture, with gridlock the most obvious finale. Governments soon saw the advantage

London to Brighton run crosses Westminster Bridge, early 1950s. (Vauxhall Motors)

of milking motorists for tax, but have never been to keen to ease their path. The Road Report for 1923 stated that the 301 single carriageway roads then being built would be adequate for all possible traffic needs for at least fifty years. It was at about this time that government first raided the Road Fund Tax for general purposes.

Pity government did not regard the wisdom of *Vauxhall Motorist* magazine in the October 1934 edition, when the editor wrote: 'Sure as fate every year round about Motor Show time, some friend or other will buttonhole us. 'Why?' he will demand, 'do motor manufacturers insist upon bringing out new models? Why can't they be let well alone...'

'The answer is simply... the world goes on. Many, many years ago on a certain memorable day, a schoolmaster said to us, 'Remember you can progress, or you can retrogress, but you cannot stand still.' The motor manufacturer is governed by that law of life as irrevocably as any boy leaving school...'

And so we have the reason why the Vauxhall Motor Company has survived the competitive world of car production. While the company has competed for markets and invested in development, the work force has competed for a growing share of the prosperity, sometimes leading to serious industrial conflict.

Given the original sounds of protest, when the decision to close the historic Luton plant became public, one might have expected industrial unrest on a grand scale. But although many marched through Luton in December 2000, most knew there was little to be done to save it. Fly posters around the town blamed global capitalism. *The Times* newspaper reported thus: 'The prospective closure of the Vauxhall car production plant at Luton – a site that has witnessed motor manufacturing for ninety-five years – is a harsh surprise compounded

An early Vauxhall Chassis, *c.*1905. (Vauxhall Motors)

by very unfortunate timing. It cannot be claimed that either productivity or
industrial relations here were unusually poor, in fact the company went to some
considerable length yesterday to note the 'considerable' improvement recorded
recently in the quality of output.'

In life there are many mysteries. Vauxhall's sister company, Bedford Commercials,
had demised over ten years earlier during those halcyon Thatcher years when unions
had to be bashed and industry become leaner and fitter. For years Bedford had
been the main military truck supplier but Leyland trucks were being groomed for
sale to DAF. A military truck contract might sweeten the pill for DAF to swallow
but it was not going to encourage General Motors to keep Bedford in business at
a time of over capacity in the European truck industry and approaching recession.
For a while Bedford would survive as AWD (All Wheel Drive).

But for the time being the future of Vauxhall's Luton plant seemed assured.
Along with other companies in the 1960s, it had been the subject of Goldthorpe
and Lockwood's 'Affluent Worker in the Class Structure' study, testing the notion
that people like car workers were so well paid that they were middle class too.
High pay, however, did not a bowler-hatted gent make, or so it seemed. The
Affluent Worker would be the first man down in a recession and resentment
would soon show itself when material needs went ungratified.

For many years, Luton, a neat little Bedfordshire town in a Chiltern bowl,
would offer hope of rising living standards to all, symbolised by the beloved motor
car. In the so called 'swinging sixties', however, geographical and labour force

AA block, one of the largest steel-framed structures of its day, built with steel diverted from a Boeing aircraft factory. This mid-1950s scene shows workers coming off shift. It is doubtful whether any of them would have owned one of the many new E type Vauxhalls or the old L type parked up around the offices. They would more likely be making for the many United Counties double deckers that used to rumble up Kimpton Road, or to the bike shed. Note the cluster of bodyless Bedford chassis, ready to be driven of to specialist coach works. (Vauxhall Motors)

constraints upon that town encouraged Vauxhall to look elsewhere for expansion. They chose Ellesmere Port, an old airfield on Merseyside, where a vast army of labour was eager to learn the skills of motor making. By 2000, Merseyside was where Vauxhall's British future lay, not in the cramped quarters around Kimpton Road, under the flight path of neighbouring Luton Airport. Having lost its hat industry and its hatchbacks, Luton seeks a new identity, but faces being engulfed in the sprawl of the government's Milton Keynes & South Midlands Spatial Study.

Fortunately, Luton has not lost Vauxhall entirely, with AA block still resounding to sound of IBC's (Izuzi Bedford Commercials) production lines and retaining the Griffin House Headquarters in Osborne Road. Vehicles are shipped in from as far away as GM Australia for distribution from Luton, where there is also a major parts facility, but it is all a long way from the company's heyday and origins. All of this change has taken place in less than 100 years and it is fascinating to walk along Kimpton Road imagining what it all looked and sounded like in those early days; thoughts making me long to time travel to meet those strangely different folk

Looking toward the redundant car factory, on the left, and IBC's plant in the old AA block, far right. (Robert Cook)

with their strange ways and bold ideas that now seem so old fashioned and out of date, who nonetheless led the way to where Vauxhall and Luton are today.

One thing is at least true, Britain is restored once more to being a major car maker, exporting cars worth £20.9 billion in 2002, comprising 11 per cent of the country's exports. By 2010 Britain's production should have overtaken the 1970s peak. Currently 70 per cent of the 1.7 million cars made here are exported. Of course, there is a catch: almost the entire industry is foreign owned, but that has been the case for Vauxhall since the 1920s. Britain is home to all the world's major car makers, thanks in no small part to the enormous contribution of Vauxhall, a company always at pains to emphasise its essential Britishness ever since the General Motors took over. Though General Motors may have been keen to play down its Vauxhall subsidiary's American links in those difficult years of protectionism, it would be wrong to diminish the beneficial influence of the United States on the class conscious snobbery of an inter-war Britain, with Vauxhall setting new standards in looking after and developing staff. In product terms, it encouraged a new and imaginative approach to the world of motor engineering, tested through motor racing and excelling in aspects of style. This book endeavours to give some insight into how all that came about.

CHAPTER ONE

A NEW CAR NOW!

One wonders what Scottish engineer Alexander Wilson had imagined his enterprise would lead to when he founded the Vauxhall Iron Works, in what became the Vauxhall District of London, in 1857. I am sure it could not have been to create one of the most successful European car and commercial vehicle manufacturers of the twentieth century and beyond.

That, of course, is the essence of enterprise: being ready to leap into the unknown, taking risks and trouble shooting all along the way. Wilson's business, looking back, seems a modest enterprise, engaged in building a variety of machines. The world of seafaring and waterways was being revolutionised by steam engines. Soon there would be another innovation: petrol-powered boats.

The company was renamed the Vauxhall Ironworks Company Limited in 1897, when a single-cylinder 5hp petrol engine was developed to power a river launch called *Jabberwock*. Others had already attached such motors to road vehicles and so Vauxhall joined in the experiment, producing their first car in 1903, powered by the same single cylinder 5hp engine. First impressions were good. The motoring press described it as 'neat, efficient and a cheap vehicle which should find many friends'. In 1903, Dr Tiffen informed *The Autocar* magazine: 'It may interest you to know that the wear and tear of driving my 5hp 1903 Vauxhall at an average speed of 15mph is almost a negligible quantity. Running costs work out at one third of the upkeep of my horse, and I have never experienced a moments worry on the road.' This unusual four seater was tiller steered with driver and passenger seated behind the other two passenger seats. A sporty looking 6hp two seater followed in 1904.

Although Wilson had left the company before the company took its new course, his chosen Griffin symbol, survives to advertise the car's Vauxhall lineage. Coincidentally, the Griffin had been the heraldic arms of Fulk de Breaute, who was probably the most evil Lord of the Manor that Luton had ever known, most fitting for the times of King John who recognised a kindred spirit. The King appointed de Breaute Sheriff of Oxford and Hertford, thus adding to the man's ignoble wealth which had already gained impetus through marriage to widow Margaret de Redvers, who had property on the Thames's south bank. That property was thence known as Fulk's Hall, eventually corrupted to Fox Hall, then Vauxhall.

A large steam engine built by Vauxhall Ironworks for a nineteenth-century paddle steamer. (Vauxhall Motors)

A forward-thinking Luton Council, recognising the decline in hat making through foreign competition, was encouraging new industry into town. By 1905, London was already congested, so with the Vauxhall company after more room, they moved to Luton, the other home of the de Breaute and his griffin. The business was restructured as 'The Vauxhall and West Hydraulic Company', with car making separated out as Vauxhall Motors Ltd, Percy Kidner sharing Managing Directorship with Leslie Walton.

Vauxhall were learning to cater for a high class market in class conscious Britain. Wealthy customers rated quality above all and Vauxhall's eager engineers approached the business rather like Rolls-Royce. Before the First World War their 35hp cars were expensive at £600. Company leadership was hands on, with young directors like Percy Kidner who enjoyed endurance driving, competing in the 1908 RAC 2,000 mile reliability trials among other events. The company's competitive spirit soon ranged further afield, even as far as Russia and Australia. Building and driving cars were very buccaneering activities, making up the rules as they went along. There were no formal requirements on how to drive, though the British School of Motoring was founded in 1910, long before driving tests.

The 5hp single-cylinder Vauxhall, of the type referred to by Dr Tiffen. Its 983cc single cylinder engine (bore 4 inches, stroke 4.75 inches) was capable of 20mph with a fuel consumption of 38mpg. The picture, from the Vauxhall Heritage Collection, shows the forty-fifth Vauxhall ever built. It was bought by a Scottish shipbuilder and after restoration, the company took it on the 1996 London–Brighton run. (Vauxhall Motors)

Meanwhile, entrepreneurs across the Atlantic were thinking of the common man and of motorised transport's potential to help unite a widely dispersed population. Henry Ford led the way toward mass production, but an equally significant force upon the US's motoring industry was going to be William C. Durrant. In 1908, Durrant was working at the Buick Motor Company when he formed General Motors as a holding company. In that year, only 65,000 cars were made in the United States. This was also the year of Ford's Model T which was selling over 500,000 units by 1916. As at Vauxhall, the personalities of the men involved became a part of and drove the more successful companies. The same was true of Vauxhall and young directors, Hancock, Kidner and Pomeroy.

However, Ford and Durrant approached matters differently and this was to have a significant effect upon Vauxhall. Today General Motors is the world's largest industrial enterprise, of which Vauxhall has for most of its life been a subsidiary. Its origins lay in the plethora of small car builders who were doing little more than attaching crude petrol engines to vehicle bodies deriving much of their design from horse drawn carriages. Not surprisingly, many of these pioneers failed, not without teaching a few lessons to competitors and sometimes leaving marginal firms ripe for the picking, to become parts of Durrants grouping. The story is

The steamer *Westbourne*, pictured during the 1960s, was thought to have been the last Vauxhall powered vessel, in service as a Port of London tug. Its triple expansion unit (14in/21½in/35in x 24in) turned at 125rpm. Along with the boiler, it was built by the Vauxhall & West Hydraulic Co Ltd in 1911 – just before the company dropped West hydraulic from its name. (Vauxhall Motors)

Percy Kidner competes in a hill climbing event up Aston Hill during early days of Luton's Vauxhalls. (Vauxhall Motors)

The author at the wheel of a sports version of the famous American Model T Ford which set the standard in the US and Britain. (John Newby/Robert Cook)

well told by Alfred P. Sloan Jnr, who, as part owner of the Hyatt Roller Bearing Company, gained a seat on the GM board when his business was taken over by GM in 1918. He wrote in his memoirs *My Years with General Motors*, 1965:

> '... survival in the automobile industry in the United States has depended upon winning the favour of buyers of new cars each year. Part and parcel of this is the annual model, the spur to which the organisation must respond or die. The urge to satisfy this requirement is the dynamism of General Motors... Growth and progress are related, for an enterprise in a competitive economy... size is only a problem of management... General Motors' long term survival depends upon its being operated in both the spirit and substance of decentralisation.'

In Britain motor cars were expensive novelties until after the First World War, but that didn't stop Henry Ford opening up a British manufacturing plant in Manchester for the Model T in 1910. In the summer of 1905, twelve men sat around a table in a small office in Temple Bar, all devotees of the horseless carriage. Their aim was to oppose and obstruct the police in the execution of their duty. Their anger had been aroused by a 20mph speed limit and activities of 'the hedgehogs'. These were two plain clothes policemen, positioned in hedgerow a furlong apart, equipped with stop watches. Another in uniform was positioned

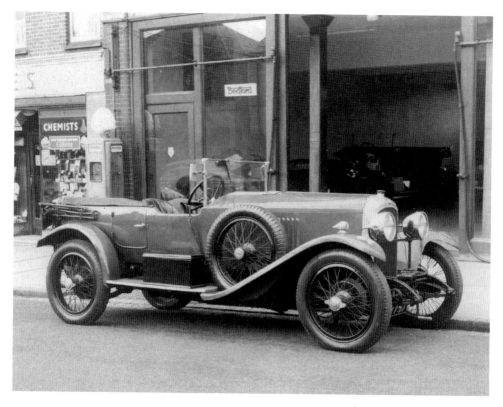

For real sports car quality, Vauxhall were hard to match. This classic 30/98 type Vauxhall first appeared in 1913, remaining a top road and track performer for the following 15 years. In racing guise it performed comfortably at 100mph on the Brooklands circuit. (Vauxhall Motors)

about a hundred yards further along in the same hedge. In the words of F.S. Groom:

> 'Three cylinders and seven horse power of juggernaut came chugging down that inviting stretch. Click went the first stopwatch, and a handkerchief waved. Two hundred and twenty yards away, another click and another wave. Juggernaut had broken 22.5 seconds – the legal maximum for the furlong.
>
> 'Spotting the second wave the uniformed one stepped out into the road and raised an imposing hand. "Stop! It is my duty to inform you..." and so on. Result is a five pounds fine for travelling at twenty and a half bit miles an hour on a perfectly safe stretch of the King's Highway!'

And so the Automobile Association was born, a crucial force for the promotion of motoring in Britain and of great benefit to the likes of the Vauxhall Motor Company.

By 1922 there were 315,000 licensed cars on British roads, Austin and Morris following the Ford example of rolling production lines. Meanwhile, Vauxhall had been more interested in making cars than money. The same was true with Durrant

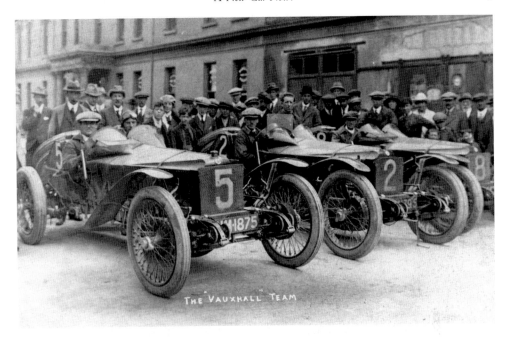

Team Vauxhall, *c.*1913. (Vauxhall Motors)

A Vauxhall competing in the Swedish winter trials in 1912. (Vauxhall Motors)

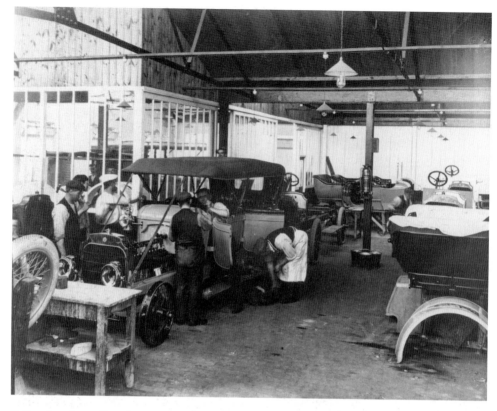

Before the advent of production lines, cars were built in batches and painting took two weeks to complete. One can easily imagine the rigours of working in this environment, but around Luton car making was an attractive proposition compared to a meagre living in depressed British agriculture. This is the original paint shop in around 1912. (Vauxhall Motors).

and his GM. Between 1908 and 1910, he bought twenty-five companies, of which eleven were car makers. Only Buick, Oakland (Pontiac), Oldsmobile and Cadillac were permanent additions as companies and divisions. The seven car makers were of interest for engineering knowledge. Durrant already had Buick making a lot of parts in house before taking over the Champion Ignition Company, renaming it AC and paying Albert Champion for his knowledge. His thinking was long term at a time when so many were pioneers were failing.

The General Motors Export Company was established on 19 June 1911, selling GM products overseas. Industry output grew from 210,000 units in 1910 to 1.6 million in 1916, most of it was Ford, with GM accounting for 40,000. Durrant's risky approach led bank borrowing up to $9 million in 1915, but dividends were good. Losing control of GM, he supported Louis Chevrolet's ventures toward developing a light car, forming the Chevrolet Car Company. Success encouraged him to increase stock in order to exchange it for GM stock as a means of regaining control – regaining the presidency in June 1916. Meanwhile, Pierre S. du Pont acquired 2,000 GM shares. Durrant transformed the General Motors Company, a New Jersey Company, into the General Motors Corporation, a

Vauxhall were always ahead of their time in caring for workers' comforts. This is the old canteen. (Vauxhall Motors)

Delaware Corporation, increasing capitalisation from $60 million to $100 million. Thus commenced the operating, rather than Holding Company, the General Motors Corporation in August 1917. Chevrolet's controlling interest in GMC was undone through buying all of its assets with GM common stock, dissolving it as a separate company and making it into another GMC Division. Durrant guided a large Chevrolet expansion programme, developing a low priced car and in, in 1919, took a 60 per cent stake in Fisher Body. Large markets were needed to sustain such a large business, making overseas outlets of crucial significance. In 1920 420,000 cars and trucks were exported, half to Britain, France, Germany and Italy. Building assembly plants in Europe gave GM knowledge of local parts suppliers, encouraging thoughts of manufacturing locally.

These were hectic times for Durrant and GMC, adding fridges, component suppliers, trucks, tractors, General Motors Canada and General Motors Acceptance Corporation to the business. The latter was an all-important means of arranging finance for expanding car and truck sales. Sadly it was not enough to keep Durrant's grand plans afloat when the trade cycle dipped. The bottom had fallen out of the market by June 1920. Durrant tried to stay afloat, borrowing to buy

Mr Boyd Edkins at the wheel of his 16–20hp Vauxhall in which he established a record for the run at 33.69mph on 18 March 1916. Proving runs across some of the world's toughest terrain were the way to earning a reputation for reliability and widening markets. (Vauxhall Motors)

shares and prop them up. Pierre du Pont expressed his concern, in a letter to his brother, that panic might ensue if word leaked of Durrant's indebtedness. The solution was a $20,000,000 loan to cover Durrant's indebtedness. Durrant resigned on 11 November 1920.

As a much smaller specialist builder, Vauxhall was experiencing life differently, though at the mercy of the same world events to some extent. Ford were gaining a strong hold on the British market, producing 6,800 of Britain's 34,000 unit output in 1913, compared with Vauxhall's 387. Austin were a little closer to the mass production league with 1,500. Reorganised as Vauxhall Motors Ltd (1914) Ltd and with capitalisation of £200,000, sales were £269, 670 in 1914 and profits £21,173. As a quality car maker, marketing was rather an exclusive business. Vauxhall chose Great Portland Street, London, for its prestigious showrooms in 1912, placing them in the hands of agents Shaw & Kilburn who continued as main dealers until the 1980s.

Vauxhall was then the directors' company. Five of them owned nearly 15,000 of the 18,000 shares in 1904. Frank Hodges had been Wilson's apprentice, taking over the drawing office and leading the way to car making. Percy Kidner and Leslie Walton shared the managing directorship and Laurence Pomeroy became chief engineer and Kidner did the car racing. Along with works driver Alfred Hancock, Pomeroy, a trained draughtsman, knew what he wanted, enlivening the scene when he became Hodges assistant in 1906, leading the way to some winning designs but not a great output. Production was confined to a quarter acre site,

The Prince Henry first appeared in the Prince Henry of Prussia Trials and the tourer became available from 1912, finding favour with the sporting fraternity and fame as a staff car during the First World War. (Vauxhall Motors)

with 700 employees. Labour relations presented few problems given the small scale and high skill nature of operations.

Vauxhall was building juggernauts by comparison with cheaper rivals. It was after power and ever more keen on competition. By 1907 the company offered a 16.8hp four-cylinder 12/14 model for £375. Achievements led to opening a Russian factory in 1911. In 1915 the magnificent Prince Henry four-cylinder packed 25hp and sold for £565.

The Prince Henry was the only wartime product, all going to the army as staff cars, along with 156 staff called up into the armed forces – 2,000 were delivered. As for industry generally, war was good for business, share values quadrupling by 1918. The peace was not so easy. The Russian factory had gone with the 1917 Revolution. The 1919 Peace Treaty of Versailles became infamous for its failures, having been much influenced by France's desire for revenge on Germany which was effectively bankrupted by the burden of reparations. The economist John Maynard Keynes was so infuriated by the settlement that he wrote two books on the subject, *The Economic Consequences of the Peace* and *The Economic Consequences of Mr Churchill*. Germany inevitably collapsed, and the United States isolated itself, heading to boom and bust. World trade went with it. But for the time being, those who would not listen to the wise had hope. Vauxhall sales slumped in 1919, the year Pomeroy left the company. Pomeroy would be missed, but his ways were out of date. War had seen many Vauxhall employees consigned to the carnage of battlefields, with those remaining working long hours to deliver orders for the

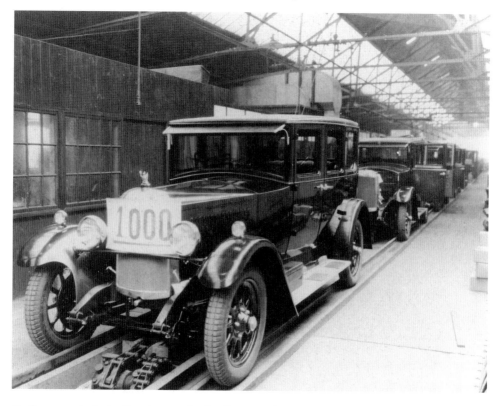

By the 1920s, the basis of modern production lines were beginning to emerge at Vauxhalls but had
a long way to go to match Ford and Austin. This picture shows the S type which was available as
a seven-seat tourer, saloon, sports saloon, limousine, landaulette and specials. The car was built on a
lengthened 30/98 frame with front hydraulic brakes and fitted with a 3881 cc sleeve valve engine. The
S type was built from 1925-27. (Vauxhall Motors)

front-line. Post-war stresses saw the tide turning and management becoming a
little anti-union as they struggled to keep the company afloat.

By 1921 there were losses of £221,758 on capital of £600,000. Looking
forward to growth, management bought another 1.5 acres on Kimpton Road,
building workman's homes and buying playing fields, all on borrowed money.
Meagre annual profits of around £40,000 kept the company afloat for three years,
followed by losses averaging around £300,000 from 1927-29. The market for cars
like the four-cylinder 30/98, at £1,960, was limited – a Morris Minor open top,
two seater cost £100.

After the carnage of war it was hard and expensive to find the skilled labour
for a predominantly craft industry. All this while, Vauxhall managers pursued their
love of car racing. They just hoped for the days when the world would go back
to Edwardian ways, carrying on regardless. From making £25,800 profit on 565
cars, using 750 staff over 8.5 acres, Vauxhall arrived at a £283,791 loss achieved
by using 1,552 staff on 11.5 acres to make 1,278 cars. Pomeroy's former assistant
and successor as chief engineer, C.E. King built the N type 14/40 in 1922 as

The innovative Vauxhall Motorcycle. Only six were built and in production would have been no
match for the cost of a mass produced Austin 7. Whatever they did, Vauxhall could not break the habit
of engineering excellence and high quality. (Vauxhall Motors)

an attempt to adapt, being somewhat more affordable at £650, but output was
far from mass market at thirty a week. Production was in batches and although
quality was outstanding, they could not match Austin or Morris on price. The
Depression was the last straw.

World events and the complexities of the General Motor Corporation
were creating problems that would make Vauxhall part of their solution. The
organisation was too decentralised. In 1920, the Board's relative newcomer Alfred
P. Sloan conducted an organisational study which led to divisions being given
as much autonomy as possible, minimising the number of executives reporting
directly to the the president. His fresh, perhaps amateur, approach, was key to
rethinking GMC. The old order were set in their ways. This was to be du Pont's
New Start, with Sloan effectively a vice president reporting directly to du Pont
– who had added being general manager of Chevrolet to his chair and presidency.
As Sloan wrote, du Pont was short on experience, but long on logic and energy.
Sloan reduced it all to the notion that every enterprise needs a concept of its
industry, such as Ford's single model. This could not be the GMC concept.
Like Vauxhall, they had nothing in the low price, high volume range and much
research was needed. The president wanted a revolutionary car. There would be a

A British Chrevolet light truck, from General Motors, of the type built from kits at Hendon, seen here preserved in an Australian Museum at Marysville, Victoria. (Sandra Condon)

product policy to cover the complete price range, with a cheap model going into mass production.

Hopefully, the cheap one was going to be a Chevrolet based on Kettering's air-cooled engine. Charles Kettering, at the Dayton Research Corporation, had already distinguished himself through work on the self starter and lighting systems. Great things were expected of him. Air cooling works by taking heat through the engine walls, using a fan to blow air over them, but this time he failed to deliver. Supporting his specific research was sound engineering policy but at odds with the new policy of seeing the organisation as a whole. Sloan observed how the research department had been preoccupied with the air-cooled engine, leaving the divisions to deal with the water-cooled. There was little room for forward engineering

General Motors recruited William S. Knusden, former Ford production manager and a dual programme of copper and water-cooled car was agreed in 1922. The following year was a boom, but the air-cooled engine proved problematic and Alfred P. Sloan succeeded to the presidency in spring 1923, with du Pont continuing as chairman. It was the case, as Sloan attests, that du Pont changed the company's psychology, laying foundations for future success – du Pont's chemical company also invented a cellulose paint that speeded up the previously lengthy process of painting car bodies.

Vauxhall LM type 14/40, built from 1925- 27. A mere 3in increase in wheelbase over allowed more coach work options over the M type. Model features included a four speed gearbox and four wheel brakes. (Vauxhall Motors)

On 6 March 1924, Sloan informed GMC's General Technical committee: 'While General Motors is definitely committed to a decentralised plan of operation, it is nevertheless obvious that from time to time general plans and policies beneficial to the Corporation and its stockholders as well as to the individual divisions can best be accomplished through concerted effort...'

Much was also to be gained by co-ordinated sales. On the operating side, the Executive Committee reigned supreme, chaired by the president and chief executive officer, with all the authority to carry out established policy. Headquarters developed fact finding and analytical techniques to forecast industry demand, along with methods to measure whether decentralised management was operating effectively. Sloan stated commercial policy in 1925: 'We have elected as a large corporation, to build quality products sold at fair prices...'

By the mid-1920s, GMC was evolving from a formless aggregation into an effective well-integrated enterprise, decentralised, with co-ordinated control and producing a variety of cars. Much of this success followed a move into England in 1925 and Germany in 1929. Sloan explained it like this: 'We expanded our merchandising operations, including overseas assembly plants and warehouses, and so brought our products closer to the ultimate consumers.' Prior to this the corporation were exporting Chevrolet Trucks in kit form for assembly at Hendon. They earned $240 million from 1923-25, returning $112 million to stockholders.

They would ride out some difficult years, expanding operations worldwide. Citroen and Austin looked like better targets for European operations, but given the former's reluctance and the financial weakness of the latter, GM had no problem working out the best deal. They were very well placed to snatch a bargain at Vauxhall in 1925.

Britain's earliest and cheapest cars were open top, but the 1920s saw a shift toward saloons with better tyres and suspension. Suburban housing estates were advancing into the English countryside, producing neat homes with tiny garages attached so that the aspiring middle classes could house their ultimate status symbol once they had arranged finance. Advertisers worked overtime to lead folk into temptation, in the name of personal freedom. Vauxhall was one of nearly a hundred firms competing for sales and in danger of collapse when General Motors came calling. Cutting prices to beat the Depression had a more adverse effect on the company's margins than on Austin and Morris with their cheap little runabouts. In desperation Vauxhall had raised a £350,000 mortgage on debenture stock, paying 7 per cent interest. There was no need for Austin to sell out to the American conglomerate, but Vauxhall would have little choice.

Although GM had solved their financial problems, world markets were crucial to sustain them. A British connection would give them access to an empire that covered 38 per cent of the globe. Also it would be possible to use Vauxhall's as a home-grown source of Chevrolet trucks, avoiding the adverse taxes payable on the Hendon output which was no more than the assembly of US-made kits. Durant had sent a group to study the European car industry back in 1919. McKenna trade barriers discouraged US imports and UK vehicle licences were based on horse power. British car tax policy used a horse power formula that favoured small bore and stroke. Since American engines featured a bore almost equal to the stroke, they were not going to be popular. Taxes, garage charges and insurance on a Chevrolet touring car in the Britain of 1925 was $250 per year compared to $138 for a British model.

Determined to build high-quality cars, mass marketing was a long way off for Vauxhall. Motorcycling was an increasingly popular alternative in motorised transport and would eventually be popular with the working man, especially with a sidecar attached. Vauxhall investigated, producing six prototypes in 1924. The closest they had so far got to popular motoring was in the development of these six prototype motorcycles, but even they were over the top, emphasising advanced engineering. The bikes had four-cylinder 991cc engines. In production they would have been more expensive than an Austin Seven! The engineers just couldn't hold themselves back and went for an advanced, and therefore costly, four-cylinder 'square' engine. The engine, clutch and gearbox formed one unit and was shaft driven with a car type clutch pedal. R.D. Thomas of Bicester acquired the only known surviving machine, built from a box of bits he bought in 1951. It took Mr Thomas until 1959 to rebuild, the frame and tank being reclaimed from salvage collection, just in time for the Vintage Motor Cycle Club's Banbury Rally of that year.

Compared to the United States, no one in Britain was into serious volume production, but Austin's 12,000 unit output in 1924 was tempting. They valued Austin at £1 million, expecting a 20 per cent return on investment. Austin wanted more and Sloan decided they were not an efficient enough organisation to bother with. Vauxhall was not well run either, by US standards, and had a financial crisis to prove it. The deal was a easily done They were producing 1,500 expensive cars a year and needed to develop a smaller car quickly. GM bought the firm for $2.5 million in 1925. Not long after, Sloan posed the question in his memoirs: 'Should we expand Vauxhall, or should we write it of as a bad investment? Was it really necessary to manufacture in Europe, or could a modified Chevrolet exported from the US, compete with cars in the European market...' Mooney, head of the export division, answered the question with the observation that the lowest priced Chevrolet cost 75 per cent more abroad. The future of Vauxhall was assured for a long time to come, expansion proceeding apace. The British empire covered 38 per cent of world markets which would greatly benefit GM over time. High unemployment during these inter-war years posed problems for chairman Charles Bartlett as he struggled to avoid dismissing too many of his staff. Labour relations were inevitably becoming more edgy in an era where left-wing militants were keen to exploit any unrest.

CHAPTER TWO

THE UNEXPECTED

Balloon tyres were still a novelty in the 1920s and 'you sent a postcard to where you wanted to stop' – brakes were that bad! Still research was proceeding apace and there were significant advances in production methods, leading to falling prices. In 1923, an Austin 7 cost £225, a year's salary to the middle classes. By 1930 it was down to £125. General Motors already had a hire purchase division, extending the idea to their British operation through Vauxhall Finance. The motor car was the way to freedom and death knell to the horse-drawn world of old. British county councils would soon be producing structure plans to accommodate the predicted needs of a growing volume of traffic. Manufacturers like Vauxhall were among those shouting for greater freedom for the motorist and better roads. Many who were not going to benefit from the spread of tarmac and motoring mayhem, protested but were unheeded. By 1929, 334,000 lorries had taken over the business of a far smaller number of horse-drawn carts doing the haulage in 1920. The First World War had been the test bed for the new technology and its end had seen the supply of tens of thousands of Army surplus trucks. But more and faster traffic movements meant more accidents.

There were no driving tests, just a few tips from someone who'd driven before. Being over seventeen was the only qualification and even that was not verified. Even eyesight went untested. Not surprisingly, by 1927 over 5,000 people were being killed in road accidents every year, with scant attention being paid to the 20mph speed limit. In town, traffic jams got worse, with grid lock already a feature of London. Traffic lights were an innovation to help the flow, but drivers could ignore them until the Road Traffic Act of 1930 made it an offence. Quite simply, transport developments were proceeding faster than preoccupied Parliamentarians or those with vested interests wanted to keep up with.

For years General Motors' great rival, Ford, at home and abroad, had relied on European versions of their Models T and A. They too had to face facts and provide an economy model for the mass market. In Britain their answer was the Model Y. It was small, capable of 62mph, 40mpg and priced at £100. Entering the market in 1932, it sold 39,000 in 1933, reaching a 54 per cent share of the small car market by 1934. With rapid expansion came rapid death, mortality rates reaching 7,000 a year. Posing around in cars was already a British hobby, resulting in even more

A 1927 six-cylinder 20/60 tourer has had an upset, rolling down the bank, during those dangerous pioneering days of devil-may-care motoring between the wars. (Vauxhall Motors)

carnage to innocent pedestrians. The motorist was unregulated and wanted life kept that way. Protests from victims of motoring madness encouraged the issue of a draft Highway Code in 1930. Road improvements included zebra crossings, roundabouts and one-way streets. Worst of all was the institution of driving tests and a 30mph urban speed limit. Self control and discipline was not going to come easily to the speed-loving car owner.

Marketing cars as mere vessels to lumber you from A to B would make life hard for the product-differentiating motor manufacturer. Speed was all around, in the air, on the sea, on Grand Prix tracks, so why not on the highway? Speculative builders saw the potential for ribbon development along the inevitably required urban bypasses. These long straight roads were ideal for would-be Malcolm Campbells to hone their skills for many years to come. Town and city driving was another matter, with traffic demands overwhelming old street layouts. The Ministry of Transport was busy working on solutions, coming up with EVA in 1933. This stood for Electro-magnetic Vehicle Actuated street traffic controller. The conventional colour light signals regulated traffic in direct accord with traffic requirements at any instant. Consisting of three parts, pressure-operated detectors, controller and signal lights. The detector was a strip of rubber 80-90 degrees from the interchange. The controller was EVA's brain, noting the arrival of every vehicle signalled by the detector, speed and order of arrival and working the lights according to traffic density. Built by the Automatic Electric Co. Ltd, of London

Vauxhall Motorist magazine, from the 1930s, depicting the introduction of Zebra Crossings and Belisha Beacons, named after the transport minister, in an increasingly road safety conscious age. There were simultaneous efforts to pave the way for a more efficient and national bus and coach system as an alternative to motor transport for the many less well off. (*Vauxhall Motorist*)

VAUXHALL CARS
FOR 1934

LIGHT SIX
12 h.p. or 14 h.p.

Standard Saloon (12 h.p. only)	£195
De Luxe Saloon with No-Draught Ventilation	£215
Four-Light Coupe	£230

SPECIAL COACHWORK ON THE VAUXHALL LIGHT SIX

Stratford Sports Tourer ...	£240
Pendine Sports Tourer ...	£235
Suffolk Saloon	£265
Tickford Foursome Coupe ...	£265
Duple Two-seater	£225
Duple Tourer	£230
Duple Open Sports	£297

BIG SIX
20 h.p. (III inch wheelbase)

Saloon with No-Draught Ventilation	£325
Hurlingham Sports Coupe ...	£395
Romney Drophead Coupe ...	£345
Denton Close Coupled Coupe	£355
Rye Cabriolet	£395

BIG SIX
27 h.p. (130 inch wheelbase)

Grosvenor Seven-Passenger Limousine	£550

(*Deliveries of the new Big Six models will commence early in 1934.*)

Full particulars from your local Vauxhall dealer, or write direct to Vauxhall Motors Ltd., Edgware Road, The Hyde, London, N.W.9.

Vauxhall Light Six Tickford Foursome Coupe £265. Coachwork by Salmons and Sons.

Vauxhall price List for 1934.
(*Vauxhall Motorist*)

and Liverpool, one was sited in Piccadilly, while others were exported to Europe, Australia and Africa.

With a proven track record in the advancement of speed, Vauxhall Motors were not going to applaud the growing regulation of their customers. They were, however, going to need wider appeal. In 1929 they had 0.75 per cent share of the domestic car market, a market dominated by Morris with 34.8 per cent. Progress was slow, so that by 1939 they still had only 9.4 per cent compared with Morris's 24.2 per cent, but this was a significant change and Vauxhall were at last establishing themselves in a home market that had grown by 124 per cent from 1931-37. As Len Holden pointed out in his study, 'Vauxhall & the Luton Economy', Vauxhall's key to future success was a cheap popular car with extras. Price cutting was replaced by model competition and Ford went into high gear, opening their integrated Dagenham Plant in 1931. Henry Ford is remembered for, amongst other things, the quote that 'you can have any colour so long as it's black.' All that changed in the early 1920s, with inevitable benefit to Vauxhall. Black enamel had been the only possibility for high volume cars. The finishing process was slow and cumbersome, taking two to three weeks using paint and varnish. On 4 July 1920, an accidental chemical reaction in the du Pont labororatories led to the development of nitro-cellulose lacquer. A lacquer base could carry more colour pigment in suspension, thus offering brighter colours – colour had been

The Vauxhall Cadet pictured outside a neat little grocer's shop in the early 1930s, and no doubt an ideal vehicle for delivering the customers orders. This 17hp six-cylinder model was introduced in 1930, marking a new phase and the first Vauxhall to sell for under £200. The 1932 model featured semi servo brakes. (Vauxhall Motors)

very expensive up until then. The new paint sped up finishing, reduced storage requirements and costs.

The 1930s saw the beginning of Vauxhall's Charles Bartlett years and the launch of an excellent PR magazine, the *Vauxhall Motorist*. The editor wrote in the first issue:

'The decision to publish a new magazine for motorists was not taken hurriedly or lightly... we did not think we should be justified in producing just another motoring paper... however – since the introduction of the remarkably popular Light Six, in fact requests for a magazine have become more frequent... We have not started in any ambitious way, nor has our arrival been heralded by a fanfare of trumpets. But you have no idea what big plans we have for the future.'

In model design, the first sign of American influence came in the shape of the Vauxhall Cadet of 1930. This was a substantial car, offered as 17 and 26hp six-cylinder versions for under £300. Drawing on US advances and GM developments, the Cadet featured Britain's first ever synchromesh gear box, removing the burden of double declutching, thus widening the appeal of motoring driving which would thenceforth have more appeal to the 'fairer' sex. Before synchromesh, the driver had to rev up the engine or by waiting for it to slow down, before slamming into gear. The clutch had to be engaged and disengaged every time a gear was changed. The synchro mechanism was developed to regulate the speed of the gear wheels for perfect changes, necessitating the use of an idler gear. The idea was that instead of the toothed gear wheels coming directly into contact when the gear lever is moved, the first engagement is between what might be called miniature clutches. As the gear lever is moved, these clutches mate together, bringing the gear wheels to the same speed. The clutches are controlled solely by the action of a spring. If the gear lever is moved carefully it will cause this spring to 'urge' the clutch surfaces together until they have mated properly and therefore both gear wheels are turning at the same speed. The spring is adjusted so that when pressure transmitted by the gear lever reaches a certain strength the spring gives way, allowing one gear wheel to slide over the clutch and get into mesh with the other wheel. These early gear boxes required great care with the gear stick as sudden jerks caused the spring to give way too soon, allowing two sets of teeth to try and engage with the engine. Anything new fangled was going to create protests. One reader wanted to know why instructions were not available to handle the synchromesh. The magazine explained that instructions were simply not necessary. The editor advised rather smugly that there were two types of synchromesh box, other manufacturers' ones and the Vauxhall box. The former would help you make a smooth change so long as you made a definite pause in neutral, the latter would guarantee it, adding: 'The fact that no pause is necessary is a great advantage when you are changing on a hill...' Vauxhall also boasted that the Cadet was fitted with Protecto safety glass. Made by Triplex, it was also fitted to Bedford trucks. and subsequent car models.

The Light Six followed in 1933, again in two models in 12 and 14hp models, selling for £195 and £215 respectively. A fleet of 250 were driven out of the Kimpton Road factory on launch day, 14 June. The new cars were making quite an impression, as the *Vauxhall Motorist* editor reported that year:

'Every time we go to the Motor Show we think how persistently coming events cast their shadows before them. For instance in 1931 synchromesh was the novelty of the show. Visitors crowded round the Vauxhall stand trying to see and hear about the new gearbox. There were some who were superstitious: said it wouldn't last. We smiled.'

'And just as we had the 'cellulose year' the 4 wheel brake' year and so on, so this year of grace 1933 will certainly pass into history as the synchromesh year. Two years ago Vauxhall led. Now everybody's doing it.'

Those days must have been great fun for test drivers, as reported in the November 1933 *Vauxhall Motorist* story, 'Two Thousand Miles in the Alps':

'Thousands of feet above the long smooth road by which the continental tourists crosses the Swiss-Italian country in search of scenic beauty are the real Alpine routes. Hazardous winding

Light Six Coupe: not just a rugged car, but a pretty face too. Motoring was becoming more available to women who could afford it. (*Vauxhall Motorist*)

paths which few holiday motorists venture to follow; rock strewn tracks which twist and climb up into the snow-capped peaks far above the timber line.

'In such a country and over such tracks a Vauxhall 14hp Light Six saloon recently completed a 2,000 miles 'proving run'. For eleven days this new car (one of the first 14hp models to leave the assembly line at Luton) battled with rain, fog and snow at high altitudes. It had to demonstrate its suitability to export markets by climbing to the top of the European world and it emerged triumphant from one of the most formidable tests ever imposed on a small car...'

As part of an international conglomerate, Vauxhall models could develop apace. General Motors' influence was also directing the beginnings of truck manufacture. Their Hendon-assembled Chevrolets were already popular, but there were concerns that the state of international trade and US protectionism would turn the tide against them. Hendon closed in 1931, with manufacturing at Luton taking over the role. The British Empire had made a British manufacturer a special attraction, raising GM's expectations for truck sales. The six-cylinder model had been photographed driving up a flight of steps and road tested to extremes. The company were aiming for the light truck market for customers like small builders. A retired builder recalled: 'We had one of the early tippers at A.F. Walker's in

An 'all British' Bedford WTH from 1935, owned by Mr T. Freshwater of Nash, Bucks, and on display at the Bedford Gathering of preservationists and enthusiasts at Cambridge, August 2003. (Robert Cook)

Winslow. I remember it had an "All British Bedford" sticker on the back.' The reason for the name change – taken from the county town of Luton's home county – and the sticker was to distance the company from the US connection. Efforts were also made to distance the company from its parents. There were also strenuous efforts to give Luton management as much autonomy as possible.

Although Australia would become one of Vauxhall's target markets, as part of the coveted empire, GM had already moved in to the antipodes and were buying motor bodies from Holden to avoid a £60 duty on touring car bodies, acquiring Holden outright in 1931. This did not prevent the export of the doughty new Vauxhalls down under.

Back home a fascinating new world of motoring was opening up, commencing the entertaining polarisation of outlook toward the horseless carriage extant today. *Vauxhall News*, Volume 1, Number 1, got straight to the heart of the matter, under the heading 'Cars and the Woman', the *Sunday Pictorial*'s correspondent wrote the following:

'Cars have a curious effect on women. They fascinate them, so that as soon as you open the door they hop straight in, leaving you to go round to the offside and risk being run over by a motor coach. But once inside they behave as though they would rather be anywhere else.

'The average woman's conception of her husband is that he is as handsome as Clark Gable, as virile as Wallace Beery and that he is so clever that it is only jealousy that keeps him out

GM New Zealnd HQ, and we are jumping ahead of the story, to get a preview of the J Fourteen- Six, launched in 1939 and proving an ideal staff car when hostilities broke out. Production ceased in 1948 after 45,499 were made. (Vauxhall Motors)

of the Cabinet. If you told her that he cheated at bridge, shot a sitting partridge, burned down an orphan asylum or anything else which is not done in the best circles, she would not believe you.

'But once he is seated at the wheel it seems to her that whatever he does is wrong and that the other fellow is always right. She warns him that he passed that junction at 25mph without hooting, oblivious to the fact that it is the entrance to a disused gravel pit. If he sees the road for half a mile ahead, and tries to pass a man on a tricycle selling ice cream, she says "Oh be careful Henry. I know we shall have an accident."

'I wouldn't mind all this so much if she did not look out of the window every time a Vauxhall goes by and say "What a lovely car. I wish we had one like that".'

For all the carnage of those days on the road, the manufacturer had to take account that motoring wasn't about necessities. Most journeys were still taken by rail and the vast numbers of poor folk never strayed far from work and home. For those who could afford a car, proper dress was of crucial importance. Once again, I refer to issue one of the *Vauxhall Motorist*: 'Hats are particularly audacious and cheerful this Autumn. Nobody knows why they have a peak here or a loop there except that it looks nice. But in fur, in feather, in velvet, in wool, they are

The Big Six first appeared in 1934, continuing in production until 1936. As was the custom, it was available with a choice of bodies. Choice was not available for all. Women had not long gained the vote and the two pictured here seem to be enjoying their new freedom. As writer H. Pearl Adam observed through the pages of Vauxhall Motorist in 1936: ' *The provision of comfort should be the first consideration of all trades connected with motoring. Not necessarily slothful and luxurious ease, of course, but that blissful state in which body is so much at peace that we can forget the troublesome creature is there at all.*

'*That is what coach builders and upholsterers are after, with their wonderful springs and upholsterings. They want to chase away those nagging little back aches which assail a spine after a few hours of stillness. That too is what the new stretchable materials are after in clothes…* ' (*Vauxhall Motorist*)

as cheeky as a forage cap and soft as a muff. They must have no brim at the back for the motorist; they are neater without it and can be leaned back in without detriment to the general scheme of decoration. Nor will they budge if the hard weather collar of fur up rises behind them.'

To put this world of luxury in perspective it is worth considering the hardships faced by people at large. Very few had money to spare after meeting the cost of essentials. Less than 2 per cent of the population owned 56 per cent of personal wealth and a half a per cent owned 18 per cent of total wealth. Two thirds of all earners received under £2 10s a week. They were not going to buy cars! The middle classes themselves did not always have the ready cash for such a large purchase as a car. Backed by General Motors, Vauxhall offered their own finance services, regularly advertised in the *Vauxhall Motorist*, backed by persuasive prose, such as:

'It's a queer business. Some people will even go without a radiogram, or a car, or a piano, sooner than make use of facilities offered by a responsible finance house.'

'Yet why? It really is strange since the world lives by credit, and without it the entire structure that is called "business" would fall like a house of cards…

'It seems about time that we came out in the open and accepted hire purchase for what it is – a perfectly sound cog in the machinery of modern business. The last thing any reputable finance house wants to do is persuade anyone to live beyond his means. the very word "repossession" makes a motor car dealer shudder, and a hire purchase man have bad dreams...

'That's all there is to it. We know plenty of hire purchase men, and they are just like us. They smoke the same cigarettes, drink the same drinks, miss the same sitters, and use the same swear words over it. None of them looks the least like Fagin, or the villain in East Lynne.

'They earn their living by helping people like us to acquire the things we want and can afford. If by mistake, one of them sells a car to someone who really can't afford it, he kicks himself good and proper, because he's made a blunder.'

Vauxhall Motorist, 1935

The Vauxhall and General Finance Corporation Ltd was not likely to make such a blunder. In 1937 it advertised

'... a Vauxhall Motors Plan That Suits Your Pocket', explaining that 'hire purchase is now accepted by the great majority of motorists because they know it to be an established credit system advanced or used in almost every commercial sphere... Those who acquire cars usually receive their income monthly and that is why we suggest monthly repayments. As each potential owner of a car is the only one who can know what he can pay down and what he can pay each month. That is why we ask him to state his own terms. The only suggestion we permit ourselves is that he should pay as much down as possible and as much each month as he can. By these means he acquires the car more quickly... he saves charges and does not waste credit... The Vauxhall "Out of Income" plan is available through Vauxhall Distributors or Dealers.'

If the masses couldn't afford personal motoring, Vauxhall were starting to provide for the growing coach market. The first Bedford coaches were built on truck bodies, Then came the WHB and WLB pressed steel coach chassis, fourteen and twenty seaters respectively. Day trips and workmen's runs were steadily increasing demand. Bus body building was a separate industry with traditions and skills going back to horse-drawn vehicles, hence their nomenclature as coachbuilders. Bedford developed a long association with Duple.

Early coaching days were something of a free for all, until Government introduced the 1930 Transport Act. Under this legislation it was necessary to have a licence for every pre-booked excursion, unless it was confined to a private party. Too many accidents necessitated controls. A system of Traffic Commissioners was established for the purpose of issuing licences. The law was amended to allow for two kinds of public service vehicle – stage carriers and contract carriages. Stage carriers covered all vehicles carrying for hire or reward at separate fares, so there was no differentiation between buses used on regular services with fares less than one shilling and coaches used on similar longer distance services with no fare less than one shilling. Tours and excursions would be operated by stage carriers, but the legislation did not deal with the issue of pre-booked party work.

Late 1930s front cover from *Bedford Transport Magazine*, focusing on the success of Bedford Duple coaches. (Vauxhall Motors)

Vauxhall'

Introducing the Vauxhall-E̶

away with any need for kno̶

has been almost entirely eliminated
by extremely efficient double screen-
ing. The only suppressor needed is
supplied with the set, for installation
between coil and distributor.

Vauxhall engineers hold strong
views about the question of drivers' attention being dis-
tracted by the necessity of tuning a radio with the normal
type of control. The Vauxhall-Ekco radio has therefore
no manual tuning control. In its place there is a rotary
selector switch with illuminated station names. Any one of
six pre-set stations can be chosen by turning the knob
from one definite position to another. "Tuning" is
automatic and instantaneous. To change any or all of
the six stations (on the long or medium wave bands) to
which the control is set is only a matter of making a
simple adjustment.

When it is delivered, the radio is pre-set to these
stations:

1. L.W. Light.   4. London Home.
2. West Home.   5. Midland Home.
3. North Home.   6. M.W. Light.

Your dealer will advise you of the selection most likely
to give you the maximum entertainment value in the
area in which you use your car most frequently.

The only other controls on the set are a combined

VAUXHALL radio engineers began to examine the
question of car radios as soon as the war ended.
Only now, after more than two years of research
and experiment, are they satisfied that they can offer
Vauxhall owners a car radio set which is up to Vauxhall
standards.

The Vauxhall-Ekco radio is manufactured by E. K.
Cole Ltd. especially for Vauxhall cars. When it was
designed, four things were considered to be funda-
mental:

1. It must be easy to instal in Vauxhalls of all models
   and all ages.
2. There must be no interference whatever from the
   car's electrical system.
3. Owners cannot be expected to fumble about with
   the normal type of tuning control.
4. Everything possible must be done to make the
   radio completely reliable.

This is how those essentials have been achieved.

Ekco have drawn on the vast experience they gained
in building vehicle radios for the services, and dimen-
sions have been kept right down. The set, which weighs
12 lbs., measures only 9¾" wide, 4¾" deep, and 6¾" from
back to front. The illustration on the right shows how
neatly it fits in place—easily reached by driver or passenger, yet not in the way of either of them.

Receiver, vibrator and loudspeakers are housed in
the one unit. Finished in "crackle black", the set is very
neat in appearance. It fits snugly in position and there
are no loose wires to get in the way. All that is necessary
to instal it is to fasten it to the scuttle with two brackets*
provided with the set, and couple up to the car battery
and to the aerial. Your dealer can do the whole job in
a couple of hours.

Another important feature is the way in which the
interference problem has been overcome. Owners who
have been used to early types of car radio will be familiar
with all the suppressors and other devices which had to
be fitted to the electrical system, and which tended to
interfere with the engine's performance.

In the Vauxhall-Ekco radio, the need for suppression

* The brackets supplied with the set are suitable for all 10, 12,
and 14 h.p. Vauxhalls after 1938. Brackets for other models are
available through Vauxhall dealers.

When fitted the set is not in the way of driver or passenger, and yet can
be easily reached by either. Special brackets are supplied for fixing the
set to the scuttle.

132

Car radio feature from
Vauxhall Motorist, 1934.
(Vauxhall Motors)

Legislating in an area where users craved freedom of the road and voted for MPs who would give it to them, made life difficult in terms of creating order. It was a heyday for buccaneering entrepreneurs, the coach being such a flexible rival to the railway. Without the charabanc and then the coach, the working classes would rarely, if ever, have left their neighbourhoods. Thus, Vauxhall's Bedford operation was on to a very good thing in supplying the bus and coach market. All over Britain there were buccaneers ready to chance their arm in this brave new world. One such was Mr A. Livermore, of Barley, Hertfordshire. A man of many parts, farmer, dairyman and butcher, he was not going to miss a new opportunity. He started his business life as a country carrier, mainly of passengers, some years before the First World War – with a ten pound note. Using a brougham and horses, he made regular trips to the market town of Royston, about five miles away. He started farming in 1914 but lost four years in the army. When he returned, he scrapped the brougham and bought a car. As business grew he replaced car with a bus. When the first Bedfords became available, he bought one in 1931 and within a few years had four. Speaking in 1935, he said, 'I wouldn't dream of changing. The drivers all like them, and passengers who have been in the latest one say it is the most comfortable bus they have ever travelled in.' The four vehicles ran all year round, providing a regular market day service (Wednesdays

ENJOY FIRESIDE COSINESS
at the Driving Wheel

With a

Vauxhall Car Heater

THERE'S A VAUXHALL CAR HEATER TO SUIT YOUR CAR

For 10 h.p., 12 h.p. and 14 h.p. Vauxhalls
Specially designed to fit neatly under the dash. Complete with demisting nozzles, tubes and all necessary fittings. Price: £7 10s. 0d. complete. Fitting charges extra.

AVAILABLE FROM YOUR LOCAL VAUXHALL DEALER

This sign marks the Approved Vauxhall Accessory. Tested and approved by Vauxhall engineers.

FOR THE NEW VELOX AND WYVERN
Immediate delivery of the special heater designed to fit the ducts which are built in the Vauxhall Velox and Wyvern is not yet possible. All orders are being filled in strict rotation. We recommend you place your order immediately with your local Vauxhall dealer to ensure the earliest possible delivery.
Advertisement of the Parts Service Development Division, Vauxhall Motors Ltd.

A Vauxhall Car Heater brings fireside cosiness to your car in wintry weather. You enjoy a warm, equable and healthy atmosphere inside the car—as do your passengers in the back seat. Your windscreen is kept crystal clear—mistless and iceless in all weathers.

Vauxhall Car Heaters are specially designed to suit your Vauxhall. Tested and approved by Vauxhall engineers they are sold and installed by all dealers. Have a word with your local Vauxhall dealer to-day.

For many years cars were draughty and cold, making blankets and warm clothing advisable on-board extras, especially in the folding toppers. Motorists had to wait until the 1950s to see adverts like this one for the latest in car heating. This advert conjours up an additional image of just how cosy life could be when enjoying the simple pleasure of cuddles by the open glowing fire. (Vauxhall Motors)

and Saturdays) to Royston, via intermediate villages. On Tuesdays Mr Livermore provided a forty mile out and return journey to Hitchin Market as well as weekday school runs and carrying workmen to and from Bassingbourn aerodrome. There were many more operators like him and Bedford trucks were providing similar opportunities to aspiring haulage contractors.

The company unveiled a 3-ton truck in 1933 and were gaining a strong reputation for ruggedness and endurance, with examples like Messrs T. Backhouse supplying road making materials, via Bellerby Moors, to build a tank thoroughfare. Trucks were doing much to help Vauxhall find its niche in the car market, providing profits and buying time.

Successful people had money and could afford to keep on buying all the latest in rapidly improving car technology. In-car entertainment was still a bit limited, requiring 100ft of aerial to receive a signal on the car radio – ideal when stopping to picnic but not necessarily for when driving. In 1933, the Light Six accounted for 40 per cent of all British 14hp registrations in 1933 and the following year saw the release of the Big Six chassis with a choice of bodies by Grosvenor and Martin Walter Ltd of Folkestone, as well as the in-house version. Design was aimed toward efficiency, economy, simple controls and maintenance. Draught-proof ventilation was a first. Amazing how simple innovations could so please in the 1930s, as *Vauxhall Motorist* attests: 'The difference which no-draught ventilation made to comfort was uncanny... by merely turning a handle it was possible to

The Big Six at the time of the 1936 launch. It was available as saloon, drop head coupe, 4 door cabriolet, specials, BXL sports saloon and limousine (as shown) and powered by either 2393cc or 3180cc OHV engines. (Vauxhall Motors)

admit as little or as much air as one chose...' A pedomatic starter removed the need for the separate starter pedal, with the accelerator pedal being made dual control so that the driver switched on the ignition and pressed the accelerator to start. Electronics were increasingly important, the Big Six including a foot dimmer switch for headlights, stop and reverse lights protected by the Vauxhall four fuse system. The *Vauxhall Motorist* commented, 'Perhaps the finest tribute one can pay to the Big Six is that it is superior in almost every way to its predecessor, the 1933 Cadet as one of the finest cars on the road.' The Grosvenor Carriage Company offered the ultimate in luxury with a seven-passenger limousine body, described by *Vauxhall Motorist* as 'a real statesman's car... a car fit to carry Royalty, Viceroys and Governors'. The Big Six had a 130in wheelbase, 27hp, full-sized body, five permanent seats and two folding. *Vauxhall Motorist* opined:

> 'The equipment is complete, from such things as companion sets (for ladies and gentlemen) and telephone, right down to ash trays and parcel net. All cabinet work is polished walnut.'

The 1930s were an age of rapid innovation and with the clout of General Motors behind it, Vauxhall introduced many improvements to their cars, including Seri servo brakes.

The earliest brake shoes opened like a hinged bracket, forcing themselves against the inside of the brake drum, but a huge load was placed on a small section

The 1930s were equally pioneering days for aviation and here we see a Big Six Cabriolet on VIP duties carrying C.W.A Scott and T. Campbell Black leading the triumphal procession through the streets after they won the great air race. All cars in the procession were Vauxhalls, at the height of popularity in the antipodes in those days. (Vauxhall Motors)

of the brake shoe. Vauxhall's solution was the Seri servo. With this, the shoe was so hinged that when you pressed the foot pedal the shoe swung outwards – and the whole face of it came into contact with the brake drum at the same time.

Cars were still very much the male domain, though a woman at the wheel of an open topper could look most appealing. For many men it was not just image and transport, the mechanisms had a magic for them and the annual London Motor Show became something of a pilgrimage. In those non-politically correct times, it is interesting that the *Vauxhall Motorist* could carry a story in 1933, under the heading 'Storm Troops at Olympia'. The report went on: 'We feel that we ought to offer an apology to those readers who visited Olympia, but were unable to examine the Vauxhall exhibits quite so comfortably as we should have liked them to. Unfortunately we are ruled with an iron hand in these Show matters and cannot obtain more than a certain amount of space. Let's be reasonable and admit that normally that space should be adequate. But this year we were rather swept off our feet. The stand was stormed from morning till night. It was generally admitted to be to be the most popular stand in the show, and as we wandered around, it was safe that at least once every five minutes or so we would hear some Jill tell her Jack, 'Do let's go to the Vauxhall stand now'.

Such were the signs that women wanted more involvement with the cars that *Vauxhall Motorist* carried a feature on oiling without overalls and featuring a dainty well-dressed women teetering around the bonnet, in a variety of oil can-holding

FOR MEN READERS ONLY

The above photograph was specially taken to illustrate the best way of cleaning out the interior of a car.

'For Men Readers Only' feature from *Vauxhall Motorist* in 1934. This shocking image reveals that it was seen as a woman's place to demonstrate how to clean the interior of the car! (Vauxhall Motorist)

poses. The reporter observed, 'There's no blinking the fact. Chassis lubrication has always been a most unpleasant business... On the Light Six chassis lubrication has been made easy for even the least mechanically minded owner...'

Punctures presented a particular difficulty for women, and, given the state of roads and tyre technology, they were not infrequent. *Vauxhall Motorist* advised: 'SS–SSS– it can happen to all of us. A word in your ear before we start. Nobody can prevent punctures, but you can minimise them by taking a few simple precautions... if you're in traffic, try to find a quiet by street. It may mean a damaged tyre, but that's better than a damaged you'. Tyre makers were doing their best to persuade motorists that they made the tyres least likely to burst. Firestone's factory was on the Great West Road, where in their own words: '...rubber is chopped up, churned up into dough, minced, mangled, sliced and baked – to give you trouble free mileage.' Steel reinforcement was a way off, so the Firestone process simply involved immersing a one way fabric into a bath of dissolved rubber so that every thread was impregnated and encased in rubber. One had to be adventurous to trust them over great distance, but one had to be adventurous to be a motorist.

With the advent of cross-Channel motoring adventures, it was advisable that men's 'better halves' knew at least a bit about the workings of their trusty runabouts. Cars themselves were usually referred to as in the female gender. Thus one lady wrote to *Vauxhall Motorist* in November 1933:

In the 1930s, before the days of 'roll on roll off' cars like this Light Six Cabriolet had to be hoisted on and off the continental ferry. (Martin Blane)

'I thought it would be of interest to you to hear the result of my two months tour in Spain in my Vauxhall Cadet, registration WP2143.

'I took her abroad with my husband last March and cannot speak too highly of the Vauxhall's performance on every type of road and in every sort of weather. As you probably know, the garages in Spain are primitive and few and far between, so we had to depend on our own scanty knowledge. As you will see we did in all about 4,000 miles... the roads are not as good as French ones, but the people are perfectly charming and courteous. The only bother is from small boys in the better known places, who run for miles wanting to show the way to hotels in hopes of remuneration and cannot be dissuaded – they even jump on to the car. The only damage done in 4,000 miles was the breaking of the glass of a headlamp in a Paris garage – we had no breakdown at all in Spain.'

Considering how hard a Vauxhall prototypes were tested, such sturdy performance was no surprise. The Luton Plant included special machines to simulate the harshest road conditions. Cars were also tested on endurance runs around Britain. Nevertheless, however well tested, the technology of safety had a long way to go and there were many reckless and irresponsible drivers. Motoring insurance was essential and the Co-op offered it in association with Vauxhall. In 1933 'A valuable concession' could be bought for six-cylinder cars of 12-14hp at

£10 10s 0d for provincial areas and £11 6s in London and Glasgow areas. There were cumulative no claims discounts of 10, 15 and 20 per cent. Unfortunately insurance could be less reliable than the cars. On 18 December 1933, Mr Justice Maughan granted the petition of the Board of Trade for the compulsory winding up of the North & South Insurance Company Ltd. It was the third failure of an insurance company mainly interested in the motor business since the Road Traffic Act of 1930 had come into force. The judge commented: 'The real reason for this debacle is very simple: the premium rates of the North and South were far too low; and this very factor of "cheapness" further reduced the possibility of profitable working by attracting a large proportion of risks which were understandable from an insurance point of view... it is obvious that cheap motor insurance is dangerous.'

We all know that women love shopping. Well, according to Vauxhall advertising, their cars were just what a chap needed to fulfil his wife's considerable Christmas requirements: 'Once upon – and not so long ago – Christmas shopping was a very mixed pleasure. It meant fighting to get on trams or buses, fighting to get off them, dodging the awkwardly shaped presents that people were carrying, and generally living through a bit of an ordeal. Now you can just jump into the car and run around. If the wife finds she's forgotten something when she gets home – well you run around again.' Of course if you did not want to run around again, you could buy the wife a car of her own, although according to the *Vauxhall Bedford Dealers* magazine of June 1936, ownership was not exactly how they saw it in their article 'Women as *Owners* of Used Cars': 'Please note that we have italicised the word 'owners' in the above headline.' The reason is disclosed lower down.

'There is plenty of evidence that women are taking the official driving tests and are in the majority of instances being passed out as efficient drivers. This means that those who succeed want to drive and are keen to have a car of their own. Many of these are married, and one result is that husbands are looking for used cars to satisfy coaxing wives. So that is why we mention *owners* rather than buyers, because although these women will be owners, the husbands will do the buying – or paying. One difficulty is that the average house-with-garage has room only for one car, so that husbands are likely to withstand the attacks made on their purses by saying there is no room for the additional car in the garage. Yet even this resistance will be overcome by the resourceful wife, who soon will discover a nearby lock up. So we suggest that this sales field for used cars be opened by means of a letter to all customers along these lines:

'Dear Sir,

'As many wives are now keen to have a car for the daily journeys, which include taking the children to school, doing the shopping, and so on, we are concentrating on used cars for ladies.

'We have found this necessary because ladies are passing their driving tests and insisting on owning cars. As their motoring needs usually are of the short run type, a used car in good condition is ideal, and we can offer you a selection of suitable, good conditioned cars.

'In point of fact, we sell only cars that satisfy the closest investigation and we always give a written statement of condition when we sell them.

'We enclose a list of the cars available at this time and should you be thinking of buying such a re conditioned car, we should welcome a visit.

'Even if none of these is suitable, we shall be pleased to send you particulars from time to time of others that come into our hands; particularly if you let us know what you seek. 'Yours Faithfully,

'If that letter should get into a home where such a car is needed, then it might easily result in a sale. In any event, it is good general publicity for your used car department.

'We know that this demand by wives is operating and we therefore recommend this small but useful campaign.'

Cars were increasingly designed with women in mind. Novelist F.A. Beaumont informed *Vauxhall Motorist*, in December 1933:

'women should be grateful for the motor car. I am writing a novel which begins with love in the nineties. The boy and girl live in the country and they are twenty miles apart. Whenever he wishes to see her, he has to cycle the distance on a cushion tyred bike. I am hoping that readers will sympathise with my hero and praise his fortitude and perseverance... to grant men a due need of praise for the endurance of courtship in the days before the motor car... Love making, even if our tempers had been equal to the strain, was quite out of the question... a point that I and many other husbands would recommend to the consideration of every manufacturer. A special immovable mirror is needed in every car, whereby a woman can make up her face. As it is, in nine cases out of ten, she will use the moveable driving mirror...'

The *Vauxhall Motorist* left no stone unturned when it came to encouraging people out onto British roads, asking the question in November 1933, 'Why not winter picnics?' Going on to explain:

'Now that the roads are being so much used for business there are hundreds of motorists who do not want to stop for a hotel luncheon, even if they can arrange to be near a hotel during economical hours. There are also many days in winter when an out of door lunch is not only possible but attractive. Only of course if one wants to get away from the lettuce and lemonade gambit. One wants something unexpected, something witty to eat, whether it is to be absorbed alone or in good company. Let us consider the winter picnic under its three aspects: hot, cold and finger eaten.'

On the matter of 'finger eaten' the magazine advised:

'Naturally they must be mostly sandwiches, but they need not be railway sandwiches. Cut the bread and butter and press it together in its original loaf shape, wrap it well, and carry it that way. Carry the filling separately. It means the merest dash of work at lunch time...'

But for the Vauxhall car makers, in all their various departments, life was no picnic. By the end of 1933, the year that Luton got its first conveyor belts and saw the end of batch production, around 10,000 cars had left the factory. The success of Light Sixes would see output double to 20,000 during the following year. For all its quaint charm and apparent diversions, the *Vauxhall Motorist* Magazine was a sophisticated sales device. With Christmas 1933 approaching, the magazine carried the item:

'I Want a New Car Now! I am a woman and I want a new car. I also want a new hat and a lot of other things, but most of all I want a new car. I said as much to hubby. He stared as men do when a woman seems to want something unusual and unreasonable- like water in a restaurant or a night by the fire. They can't understand women because they expect them to be freekish. That's the oddity of it all. We women are frightfully logical... And that is why I want a new car. Winter is the time for new cars...'

CHAPTER THREE

MORE INDIVIDUALITY

Why is there no throttle control or ignition control on the Vauxhall steering wheel? This was a question posed for the *Vauxhall Motorist* magazine in December 1933. One might imagine that this was a reference to cars being driven with so little attention to the control of speed when the editor replied that 'none was necessary'. Happily this was not so, but merely to do with yet further advances in design. The choke had been connected in such a way 'that when you pull the choke control you automatically set the throttle in the best position for easy starting... So far as the ignition is concerned, the control is entirely automatic...'

As with anything automatic, there was much complexity behind it. The spread of motoring was unleashing complexity everywhere, rather as computers did years later, by speeding up communications and developing markets. Again, like computers, there were fanatics who would have liked to put a stop to the whole business which had started so inauspiciously under control of the Red Flag Act.

In modern car-mad Britain, it is hard to imagine the level of hostility expressed by so many toward motorised traffic. The editor of *Motor* was thus impelled to defend his fellow drivers in December 1933:

'Powerful influences are engaged in efforts to bring about repressive legislation aimed at curtailing the fullest possible extent to the free use of private motor vehicles by penal enactments against individual motorists. These influences have been active in the press and on the platform. They are reflected in recent efforts in Parliament to pass drastic legislation which in the case of the motorists... will subvert the whole structure of the common law of England by penalising one section of the community...'

The article complained that some motoring infringements could lead to imprisonment, whinging that:

'No legal obligations attach to those who walk. They have freedom of action which they often exercise foolishly and dangerously at their own risk and at the risk of others. The law as it stands at present, is one sided and the scales are adjusted to weigh unfairly against the motorist. The motoring community will pay in taxation in 1933, a sum of approximately £66,000,000 to the state – that is about one tenth of the national income. The money so

Every half-minute or so they darted into the traffic.

Cartoonist's impression of F.E. Bailey's observations in *Vauxhall Motorist*. (Vauxhall Motors)

obtained is used for general revenue purposes for derating in the interests of other industries and for roads. The distribution of this huge sum is as follows: Taken by the Treasury apportionment and the rating relief together £5,000,000, etc., £37,000,000 on roads.'

The author felt that more should be spent on roads and that the high accident toll was due to Victorian lighting and bad planning of arterial roads and bypasses. During the fourteen previous years, 2 million people had been killed or seriously injured – half of whom were pedestrians. Policing motorists was challenging. As novelist F.E. Bailey wrote, in *Just a Few Lines to a Policeman* (1934):

'For your patience, courtesy and efficiency I have the greatest admiration and I think it would do any motorist a lot of good if he had to put in a couple of spells a year on traffic duty at an intersection of two busy streets. He would probably find himself in court on a charge of attempted murder or at least common assault...'

Vested interests of the motoring industry were undaunted, the editor of *Autocar* writing in 1934:

'While I can fully appreciate the pressure which resulted in the Minister of Transport proposing a 30mph speed limit in built up areas, I do not think that the limit is likely to have a very beneficial effect. The only reliable statistics we possess regarding the prime causes of road accidents are the figures in the report dealing with road fatalities last year. The most outstanding fact which emerges from that is that in only 685 cases out of a total of 7,001 casualties was the pace of the vehicle to be the main or even a contributory cause of the disaster... a large proportion... ccurred in built up areas. Out of 6,657 cases, in which an estimate of speed was given, in rather over 4,000 instances the estimated speed of the vehicle involved did not exceed 20mph.'

Editorial, in February 1935's *Vauxhall Motorist*, opined that:

'...nine motorists out of ten will not worry about the new speed limit until they are caught for doing 35mph in a deserted wide thoroughfare that happens to be scheduled as a built up area... the motoring organisations protest but the voice of the individual owner is never heard, is is a whisper that may be a roar before many moons go by. It is the voice of two million bemused motorists and their familles who are stung by unspeakable injustice... We seem to have no valid defence in the eyes of some pedestrians or those cyclists who wobble their way with only a dirty reflector to show where they are...'

The editor of *Vauxhall Motorist* was still at war with the speed limit in March 1935, commenting:

'As our cover this month jestingly reminds you, on March 18th we must welcome back the speed limit. Our attitude toward it is unchanged. We don't think it will prevent any accidents. If the existence of the limit meant that every motorist would be forced to slow down in built up areas then accidents would undoubtedly be reduced... But of course it will not mean anything of the kind. You and we will continue to drive with due care and attention, the reckless road hog who is showing off to his girl, the fellow who has had just enough to drink to make him think he is smart – these will continue to 'blind' limit or no limit. And these are the motorists who have accidents...'

Minister of Transport, Hore Belisha said:

'Pedal cyclists constitute the major part of the problem of road accidents. What are we going to do about it?'

Part of the answer to accident prevention, in 1934, was standardised and unambiguous road signs. Tyre advances were also crucial, with Goodyear advertising 'Double safety against skids and bursts'. Breakdowns often caused accidents and Vauxhall engineers calculated that 80 per cent of breakdowns were due to faulty lubrication. From the earliest days, the company recognised and advanced the causes of safety and sound maintenance, making their products popular with the media stars of the day. When radio star Teddy Brown was asked in a Vauxhall advert, how long he had been a motorist, he replied, 'Ever since I have had a chauffeur!'

Chauffeurs were all well and good if you could afford one. Otherwise it paid to know lots about workings under the bonnet. To assist in this matter, *Vauxhall Motorist* published many articles, on almost every aspect, in question and answer form, such as 'Why have a big air cleaner?' 'Why have a starting pedal instead of a button?' 'How to get nice fat sparks!' 'What is the idea of a crankcase ventilator', and 'Let's have a look at the valves'. The advice was detailed and well illustrated because one never knew when you might need to know. The language of explanation was full of thirties' charm:

> 'you might as well go indoors and put on an old suit, or overalls if you have them. It isn't a dirty job, but you can't dodge oil entirely when you're working on a motor car engine. While you're indoors, get an old newspaper. Tell you why presently. All set? then raise the bonnet on the offside – the side you sit when driving- and open the tool box. Get out the tool kit, and select from it a spanner to fit the two chromium plated nuts on top of the valve cover. Put the tool kit open on your bench...'

Vauxhall's advice ran for pages every month and was always most encouraging:

> 'Many an owner runs down his car because he thinks he can adjust tappets by guesswork... Although patience is needed, it is a fascinating job...'

The publishing team had plenty of expertise to back them up, including, in 1934, T.H. Wisdom,

> 'the famous racing and rally driver whose performances on roads and tracks under severe competition conditions have made him the complete motorist. The great and growing motoring public is his principal interest...

The aptly named Mr Wisdom, who was also motoring correspondent of the *Daily Herald*, pointed out that:

> 'With the modern type of engine it is not only unwise and harmful to warm up slowly, but it is most desirable to get the engine to the normal running temperature as quickly as possible...
> 'Briefly it has been established that the existing theories about cylinder wear are wrong. the wear is not caused nearly so much by the physical action of abrasion as by the chemical action of corrosion. And the corrosion is definitely caused by certain deposits which settle on the cylinder walls only when the engine is not properly warm... In the old days the oil was thick and sticky in cold weather, and didn't get where it was wanted until it had become fluid enough to be splashed (or squirted) about freely. But modern oils are fluid at all temperatures and the Vauxhall lubrication system so efficient that provided a good brand and the right grade is used all parts of the engine get all the lubricant they need as soon as the engine starts to run...'

The popularity of caravanning added another dimension to the world of the complete motorist. A feature in *Vauxhall Motorist*, April 1934, suggested that:

'Caravanning isn't so very difficult. Many private cars are now used to draw light trailers of various kinds. The caravan holiday is increasing in yearly popularity and caravan owners and hirers will of course remember that trailer caravans are in every respect subject to the general law as to trailers. Only one trailer may be drawn by a private motor car and the distance between the car and the trailer must not exceed 15ft. The maximum trailer size is 27ft and a width of 7½ft. Caravaning is contagious. We catch it from our friends and thereafter it just grows.'

Indeed it did, with great benefit to Vauxhall Motors. In those early days there were some odd designs for in-car sleeping, such as the 'carabed' which attached to the flat back of the typical 1930s limousine, pulling out concertina fashion when the car was parked up, and advertised for those who did not want a caravan proper. Vauxhall was keen to encourage caravanning, with pages of advice in its magazine, and eager to encourage new blood with these words:

'When towing for the first time one may feel conscious that the caravan is asserting its presence unduly, but this feeling gradually wears off to such an extent that on a level road the driver may even forget the existence of the caravan. Then you need to be careful!'

If the 1930s motorist wanted cheap touring without the burden of towing a home from home, there were the roadhouses. The manager of such a place informed *Vauxhall Motorist*:

'In only one season I have learnt the ropes of the road house business. I have entertained world famous people at weekends. I have witnessed many sweet romances and 'sub rosa 'love affairs. I have learnt what a fortune can be made from running a road house... have supplied maiden ladies with coffee in the mornings... superintended midnight bathing parties... it's all part of the job... The swimming pool has paid for itself twice over. Young men and women come down from the West End on hot evenings and love a plunge into the illuminated pool. I have read stories of "daring" bathing parties at the seaside, but I can assure you that in a properly regulated road house there is nothing at which even the most susceptible can take offence. In fact it might easily be a municipal pool...

Once we had a police raid. A Mother Grundy of the watch committee had complained of the number of young people who seemed to be scantily clothed! A car load of very red-faced 'speed cops' drove up and ordered all moonlight bathers on parade... Names were taken and I was interested to see that one of the young ladies featured in a recent breach of promise case... against the man she was bathing with on the night of the police raid!

'Often I see a police detective dancing and enjoying himself with the crowd. He comes to see that we serve drinks in a proper manner. You see, we haven't a real licence, and for a long time we have had a motor cycle squad... two bright lads out of a job offered their motorcycles as a sort of patrol to keep up communication with a public house about a mile away. Now when a customer orders his drinks, the waitress's slip is rushed to one of the waiting motorcyclists, who dashes off down the road with a basket strapped to the pillion! He is back in less than four minutes with the order... and we still have to keep on the right side of the law!'

Motoring opened up a world of opportunity and Vauxhall journalists reported every aspect. If a girl was going to get invited to one of those road house soirees, she had to be a pretty passenger. H. Pearl Adam was on hand to help the flirty thirties girl. Her 'Dress Comfort and the Car' feature showed Miss Vauxhall (spring 1934) reclining on the offside front wing of a Light Six, wearing a Nicoll suit of Lastex stretchable yarn, recommended by Miss Adam because it offered 'freedom of movement and sport spread'. She elaborated thus:

'The provision of comfort should be the first consideration of all trades connected with motoring. Not necessarily slothful and luxurious ease, of course, but that blissful state in which the body is so much at peace that we cannot forget the troublesome creature is there at all. That is what coach builders and upholsterers are after, with their wonderful springs and upholsterings. They want to chase away those nagging little back aches which assail a spine after a few hours stillness. That too is what the new stretchable materials are after in clothes. In the undergarments – well, if it doesn't exactly spring to the eye (though so many undergarments do nowadays), the usefulness is apparent...'

In a later feature Miss Adam looked at the virtues of wool and motoring, with two elegant ladies posed before a splendid Big Six:

'Molyneux's grege woollen get up is a peach. The dress is in soft tweed with diagonal weave, coming cosily high around the neck, when it fastens with a big natural pig skin, matching the belt. There is some dark deception about this dress. It looks like a jumper and skirt, but it is all in one....

Times were changing, though, the large cars that had made the Vauxhall's name were a passing breed, but a whole new world of possibilities was opening up.. In April 1934, company chairman Leslie Walton was able to announce much good news a the AGM:

'Compared with last years figures... the sales have increased by approximately seventy per cent in units sold... last years was a good year for trade... The number of motor car registrations in the United Kingdom reached a total of 186,543, the highest number of registrations on record for any year and representing almost a twenty per cent increase over 1932. Commercial vehicle registrations reached a total figure of 58,754, an increase over the previous year in terms of units of fifteen per cent.'

Walton went on to say that they expected the Light Six to do well and it had been well received by the press. The car, he said:

'can only be described as a complete success, and was one of the prime reasons for the very heavy strain placed on our production facilities, particularly in the latter part of the year. The limiting factor to sales has seemed to be so far, our inability to meet demand... increasing demand for the 17hp Cadet... indicating to my mind, that trade is showing definite signs

The Light 6 would set a more modern trend. This fine example is making light work of a steep hill in open country. (Vauxhall Motors)

of revival... again turning to the roomier and bigger type of car, so that the Olympia show last year introduced a 20hp model which will be known as the Big Six to replace the 17hp Cadet...'

The Big Six would be the last of a kind, reviewed by an in-house engineer as an experience in luxurious motoring:

'The car placed at my disposal was luxurious; the roominess and finish of the body were certainly most luxurious and the smooth and silent and comfortable cruising was luxurious. Yet I learned that the price of this car – the new Vauxhall 20hp Big Six saloon – is only £325. It is a thoroughbred from stem to stern, whatever the rate of travel there seems to be a complete absence of drumming. It is possible to hold a conversation with the rear seat passenger. At the other end of the scale the good slow running is very pleasing... so too is the entire absence of pinking when pulling away on full throttle... This big car feel of which one is all the time conscious, was even more enhanced in my mind by the marked stability of the car of the car under the most severe tests...'

The no draught ventilation system already popularised by the de luxe Light Six came in for a good deal of praise and the luxurious nature of the upholstery and interior fitments was much admired. Vehicle tax was rated on horsepower and was then set at £15 for the Big Six – a lot of money then. The 1933 Road Traffic Act distinguished between tax for private and goods vehicles, but private motorists could carry goods as long as they did not modify their vehicles.

Leslie Walton said that demand for commercial vehicles and Light Sixes made it difficult to build enough Big Sixes:

'On the commercial side the various types we produce up to two tons have been sold to every type of user of such vehicles. Our plan of studying the requirements of each trade and meeting them, has undoubtedly resulted in our receiving orders from those firms who might study reliability and economical running.

'Every indication points to still better business, especially in the British Dominions and Colonies where undoubtedly our products are meeting with a very big demand. apart from the financial results of last years working, I think we can look back on 1933 with a great deal of satisfaction; we have gone steadily forward to attain certain objects as part of our carefully worked out policy... Before concluding, there is just one other matter which I would like to mention. I feel I must make some reference to the fact that our Vauxhall cars and Bedford trucks are as near 100 per cent British in material and labour as it is possible for any motor vehicle to be here in England. I make this statement deliberately because it must be obvious to any understanding Englishman that there are several items of raw material in any English car that are not produced in England and cannot claim the label '100 per cent British'. Such items as copper, rubber, cotton, etc., would manifestly find difficulty in claiming an entirely British origin and the list could obviously be further extended. I am compelled to refer to this point because we have undoubtedly suffered by statements made by apparently interested parties that even such items as engines, axles and so on are imported into this country and assembled by us at Luton...'

Sales of Vauxhall Bedford vehicles were indeed impressive in 1933, totalling 27,636, compared with 16,329 - in 1932. Luton was building 150 chassis per day, with a continuing and massive investment programme. Flash welding accelerated body building massively. Leslie Walton was understandably full of thanks for Luton Corporation:

'It is a pleasure to pay tribute to the great helpfulness of the Luton Corporation and its officials generally; without whose help and co-operation our rapid manufacturing expansion would have been a problem of the greatest difficulty...'

General Motors ability to support credit purchasing, through their Acceptance Corporation, was great for sales. From 1933 to 1938, the production area was expanded from twenty-one to fifty-eight acres, including the construction of K block. A three shift system kept the new production lines rolling night and day by the end of the thirties.

New methods in the mid-1930s, made cars faster, more reliable and relatively cheaper. New houses had to make room for the middle classes 'must have' motor.

On behalf of *Vauxhall Motorist*, H.J. Kaye wrote :

'If you are thinking of building a garage... where possible the... site should not be exposed to prevailing winds and should get the benefit of the morning sun so as to house the car warmly.'

In the same October 1934 edition, Demetrius Colpuddle wrote:

'Passengers are very small beer in these days... Being a passenger, I notice that I do not occasion a big financial noise even among the manufacturers. Strangely enough a car holding three or (if they squash up) four passengers is priced very little higher than a car holding only one passenger. It may even cost less, on the grounds that a car constructed to hold only one nice girl passenger is worth more to a sound thinking man than a car which permits her to bring her mother or her chaperone along...'

This was a very literal world, a long way from the political correctness of today. Product differentiation and gadgetry led to a boom in advertising, but car technology was still crude by today's standards and adverts had story teller's charm, as with this example from October 1934:

'You don't seem to worry about your car, old man'. 'My dear chap! I worry about it in the only practical way. Worrying about your car will not stop it freezing. *"Stop it Freezing"* will (ingredients include distilled glycerine)'.

On a more sombre note for the freedom-loving motorist, there were to be driving tests from 1934. The *Vauxhall Motorist* editor commented:

'the new tests for motor drivers may seem all right in theory, but the modern car is practically foolproof, and anybody over the age of ten and under a hundred ought to be able to start up, change up, turn a corner and stop and unless he suffers from stage fright while undergoing his examination. But the ability to do these things does not make a perfect driver.'

This same writer was shocked to find himself at the mercy of a female examiner in May 1935, but he recalled the experience without prejudice:

'It was recently announced that out of 5,003 candidates examined in the two weeks ending March 30th, 4,665 passed.'

In other words, ninety-three out of every 100 were successful. He quoted sample questions posed for him by the lady examiner:

'What is the major road ahead sign, describe it to me?... Describe the types of level crossing signs and explain the difference.'

Answering the last question thus:

'Gates on the sign indicate a crossing with gates. A puffer shows that there are no gates.'

His examiner responded:

'You are only the second person to answer that. Well on your oral exam you have done quite well. I have purposely given you what I call unusual questions because I expected the editor of the *Vauxhall Motorist* to be fairly well up in ordinary road signs. For a complete beginner my questioning would be less severe.'

The editor went on to write:

'The examiner congratulated me on not having left the car outside the office where there was a no parking sign, although there was enough space to tempt the unwary... I drove with my customary care... Presently we approached a railway bridge over a road. "Pull up exactly within the shadow of that bridge" she said. 'I pulled up nicely and without jerks... "You are 18 inches from the kerb and you should be no more than six inches..."'

As you would expect, the editor of *Vauxhall Motorist* found the test:

'Dead easy... not nearly so difficult as the one I had to pass in 1916 with a WD (War Department) lorry.'

By 1935 there was a complete new world for the motorist and the British Motorist was a most complete person, passengers and all. Demetrius Coldpuddle went even further in his ideas of a complete motoring lifestyle. Roadside garages sprang up along trunk roads and in the smallest villages, where blacksmiths hurried to embrace new skills and customers. Home maintenance appealed to many men and Vauxhall exhorted them to beware of cheap fake parts. In 1937 the company's chief chemist and metallurgist, H.S. Bavister, wrote a report entitled 'Inquest on a Substitute Part'. It concerned testing replacement parts to destruction:

'Not only do we, but all other manufacturers urge him (every motorist), for his own sake, not to run risks by buying imitation replacement parts. the argument is that genuine parts, made in precisely the same way and conditions as new vehicles, must be safer... we in the laboratory at Luton might be described as the official "testers". We examine everything that goes into the vehicles the factory produces. Not long ago we took two axle shafts, one genuine, the other a substitute, bought on the open market, just as you might buy it. We took drillings from each and analysed them in the "lab". Here is the result of the chemical tests:

Substitute Shaft	Production Shaft.
Carbon 0.6 per cent	0.28-0.34 per cent
Nickel Nil	2.75-3.50 per cent
Chromium Nil	0.50-0.80 per cent'

The *Vauxhall Motorist* editor practices his reverse while the lady examiner judges his competence according to the standards of a new driving test. Note the art deco hood ornament and the way that wipers swing from above the screen on this Light Six. Wire wheels also cut rather a dash. (Vauxhall Motors)

The chemist went on to explain that an axle requires a tensile strength of 65-75 tons per square inch, so a shaft of a four square inch sectional area would need 260 tons to break it. Plain carbon steel, however, is not tempered and hardened to such a strength. Heat hardening of parts had become such a major aspect of car-making that, by 1938, Vauxhall were using 1,500,000 cubic feet of gas every week. The object of the exercise was to increase hardness and durability. Without the process, gearboxes would have to have been three times larger and heavier. A gudgeon pin needed nine hours' treatment in 1938 and a speed driven gear four hours, both at different temperatures. They were cooled, inspected, re heated and quenched in oil or water, depending on the metal.

Writing in the March 1935 edition of *Vauxhall Motorist*, Coldpuddle suggested:

'Many people contend that even a car... is not complete without a dog. and let me say they are quite right. For one thing a sturdy, well-dentured bull dog is as useful as most anti-car thief devices. More so in fact, because a fellow whose gents trousering has been transformed into a distressed area is apt to attract public and police attention.'

Police attention was becoming more and more a force to be reckoned with. As *Vauxhall Motorist* reporter Kent Barnet explained in 1936:

Two of the not so ordinary police cars featured along with Kent Barnet's article on Renfrewshire County Constabulary – namely Vauxhall's Light and Big Six. (Vauxhall Motors)

'Men of the Mobile Police may spend hour after hour at the wheel in dull monotony... checking up minor road offences... keeping an eagle watch for the number-plates of stolen and dangerous cars. Then suddenly comes the thrill. The operator of a radio-equipped police car will get a message flashed to him, or the driver of a disguised van will pick up a phone message from a police box... called to it urgently by a flashing red light. A chase may take the detectives anywhere... may end in a crash head-on; for the mobile officers, like every other section of the police, have to get their man. The ordinary cars of the mobile squad are not specially built for ramming bandit cars, but, but in emergency a driver would have no hesitation in ramming a car or forcing it into the side of the road.'

The ordinary cars pictured with this article were not ordinary at all, of course. They were the Vauxhalls; Light Six and Big Six, outstanding motors of that age. Not surprisingly Vauxhalls would become a traditional choice for British police forces.

There was an increasing range of car accessories, though radios required the car to be stationary so that 100 foot of aerial wire could be deployed – though by 1938 the problem was solved by inventions such as the Master Radio, at 13½ guineas. Since car owners were out to cut a dash, as every self respecting chauffeur knew, the best car polish was Wilcot's. More useful items offered in the 1935 Jubilee year were Lucas trafficators and a clip on tyre gauge. Many preferred to lay the car up during difficult winter months and Vauxhall offered detailed advice on the procedure. For those keen or forced to brave the 1930s roads, in 1937 Lucas offered the aid of their FT 57 fog lamp for 57s 6d. Advertising material explained that this was:

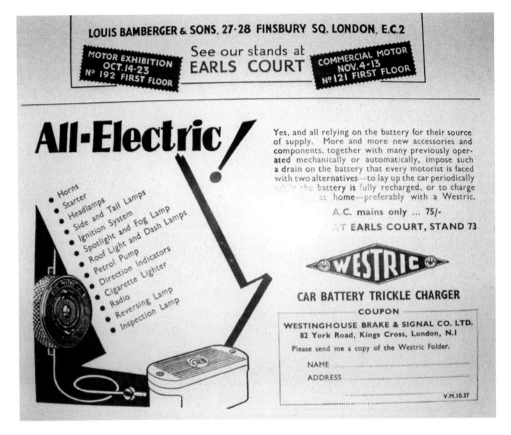

Advert for Lucas Trickle charger, 1930s. (Vauxhall Motors)

'based on the well tried Lucas flat topped beam, 'having a shallower bowl-shaped body of graceful modern outline, specially designed for the latest model cars where frontal space is restricted.'

The peculiarly British world of motoring one-upmanship was on its way. The best way to make yourself stand out was with a special body, as *Vauxhall Motorist* observed in April 1935:

'One of the most interesting features of the last motor show was what the Stock Exchange would call the 'marked liveliness' in special bodies. There are always some motorists who want and are prepared to pay for 'something different'. We have often been told by an owner that he wants a Vauxhall – is determined to have a Vauxhall – but at the same time he wants a car with more individuality than the standard model...'

Advert for Lucas Accessories, 1930s. (Vauxhall Motors)

A 1930s tyre-making feature from *Vauxhall Motorist*. (Vauxhall Motors)

CHAPTER FOUR

THE SENSIBLE WAY

The 1930s had style, at least for those who could afford it. The *Autocar* offered a more objective assessment of the Big Six in September 1934:

'There is undoubtedly room for British built cars of about 20hp with their reserve of power and effortless running at quite high speeds. It seems possible that as a result of conditions generally and the forthcoming twenty-five per cent reduction in the scale of taxation, cars of this size are likely to gain in popularity in the near future. An example is the 20hp Vauxhall, which it will be remembered, appeared at the last Olympia Show. Features of the equipment are a wide, folding, centre arm rest for the back seat which can adequately take three passengers, a footrest for the back passengers, a roof net, cubby holes, unusually deep door pockets and two roof lamps. These light up when either rear door is opened... A system of automatic car chassis lubrication supplies the principal bearings and is operated by engine suction.'

Meanwhile 45 ton girders were manoeuvred into place, linking existing factory buildings with new ones, in a race to expand the factory, the original island site having been fully developed. The phenomenal rate of the company's growth is evidenced by comparing payroll figures of 1,960 in September 1929 with 6,200 in September 1934. For every 100 units being produced in 1929, over 2,000 were being produced in 1933. By the end of September 1934, Vauxhall had beaten the production figures for the whole twelve months of 1933. Expansion posed enormous difficulties, involving excavating tons of earth from the surrounding Chiltern Hills. American thinking was in the direction of an integrated car making plant, and Vauxhall still lacked their own foundry. British car factories had grown ad hoc, responding to market influence, not through forward planning. Albert Kahn started the trend for over styling factory buildings, training in Detroit, where he inevitably moved into car plant design, setting a standard which GM would want to follow in their British establishment. Pevsner's *Architectural Guide to Bedfordshire* summarised Vauxhall architecture thus:

'The Vauxhall Motor Company came to Luton from Lambeth in 1905. It turned to motor cars in 1907...The offices in Kimpton road are by H.B. Cresswell, 1907-15, neo-William-and-

In 1934 Vauxhall announced that it would have to expand either by crossing the railway line or Kimpton Road. The company chose the latter, using massive 45 ton girders 92½ feet long and 9½ feet high, to build a bridge to connect the new and existing plants. The new building would overshadow all others; assembly lines little short of half a mile would run the length of it. Those girders and construction work are shown here prior to the extension link's demolition in the 1980s. (Vauxhall Motors)

Mary, of brick with quoins and a doorway with a big semi-circular pediment. Extensions in the same style. The main factory building is by Howard Fairbairn & Partners, 1957–58. It covers 1½ million square feet.'

Jumping ahead in the story, it is worth noting Pevsner's reaction to later developments:

'The most recent building is the STYLING CENTRE, by the same architects, 1962–64. It is itself irritatingly overstyled. A long four-storeyed facade, all forward and backward in saw tooth fashion, with resltless pre cast concrete members. The porch is big enough for Gog and Magog to call.'

Within the new buildings, great advances were underway. New model development was and still is a complex process. In the 1930s and for many years after, it began with a drawing, developing into a clay model and then into a full sized imitation car, known as a mock up. The mock up included seats upon which sat the directors, the body experts and anyone else intimately connected with the development, trying them out in every conceivable position.

In the experimental department a number of actual cars were built to the Chief Engineer's designs. Expensive necessities, these pre-production cars were taken out on the road with disguised radiators and dirty coach work to be driven out at nightfall until dawn by special drivers for thousands of testing miles, returned each morning along with copious notes about braking, acceleration, road holding and general performance.

During the mid-1930s, wheels became smaller with fatter tyres and a new system of independent front suspension designed by Dubonnet. This revolutionised the old system where, under heavy braking, the front of the car would nose dive because the whole front axle assembly was one unit. This also had the effect of throwing wheels out of the vertical every time they hit a bump. The new front independent suspension meant that each wheel could ride over obstacles whilst retaining its track and give a much smoother ride. Conventional springing of the day, because steering springs were short and stiff, required the front axle to be separate from the chassis and joined by springs. Part of the steering was on the axle and part on the chassis, therefore stiff springs were needed to restrict movement. Consequently, when a car hit a bump the front rose up and the back, with much softer springs, went down, quite a long way. The Dubonnet system overcame this problem because independent springs needed no separate axle and could therefore have softer springs to absorb the shock and the whole front of the car did not go down. The Vauxhall Light Six was among the first to benefit from this innovation, along with a redesigned cylinder head and new vacuum ignition control. The entire engine floated on rubber, obviating metal to metal contact between engine and frame. The new Light Six chassis was cross braced, giving lightness and rigidity and complete with synchromesh gear box. The Vauxhall Super Synchro gear box involved a checking device to prevent gear wheels coming together until their speeds were synchronised.

Some indication of Vauxhall's rate of progress can be gleaned from the letters pages of the *Vauxhall Motorist* in March 1935. Horace Bartford of Luton informed the magazine that he was the first Lutonian to buy a Vauxhall when the works came to town, purchasing a 16hp, four-cylinder model, in 1909, using it to explore over 60,000 miles. His explorations included the Honister Pass in the Lake District and many passes in North Wales that had been described as impractical for motorists, causing a sensation and workmen to stop and gawp at his new-fangled contraption. Horace recalled:

'One Christmas Eve, after crossing the Yorkshire Moors, I was hailed by a policeman and ordered to join in a chase for a thief – who incidentally was caught by the Vauxhall'.

C.F. Sanderson's first Vauxhall was a 1910 Prince Henry. He wrote approvingly of his 1935 Big Six:

'Speaking with over thirty years experience of motoring, I congratulate you on having produced an extraordinarily good car at a very moderate figure. when I look back over the past I am amazed at the improvements in design, performance and price. The "20" requires so little attention that it is apt to make me careless.'

In 1934, Mr H. Kops, a motorist from Cape Town, South Africa, won a wager that he could complete the 2,537-mile trip around the Union in seventy-eight hours. His adventure and praise for his Light Six (14hp) Vauxhall was reported in the *Rand Daily Mail*. Interviewed in Johannesburg twenty-six hours into his journey, the paper reported him as looking fit and in a hurry, with little to say. His only comments were that 'Vereeningning had the worst stretch of roads in the world'. According to the report:

'Even had he taken longer on the road, the trip would have been spectacular. As events proved, however, he exceeded his own sanguine expectations, thus exemplifying not only the faultless performance of a light car over an almost non stop run but the wonderful stamina of the driver.'

Even in the comfort of a modern car, the same trip today, non-stop except for fuel, would be demanding. However, by the standards of the day, the Light Six was luxury and state of the art. No draught ventilation, improved front suspension, an electrical system featuring a three way charging device, needle roller bearings and a new progressive braking system, made the car a driver's delight on challenging terrain as well as round town motoring. Should there be need for running repairs or a wheel change, the Stevenson system of designated jacking points made the job so much easier.

Closer to home, a reader informed *Vauxhall Motorist* of his European trip in Big Six, registration FMC 999, in 1937:

'Our first destination was the Pyrenees and the route we followed was familiar to many English motorists, judging by the number of GB cars we saw. One of our stops included Bordeaux and as the garage at which we left the car had an official Tecalamet sign up, we decided we might as well make use of this world-wide service. We were interested to find that the charges are based on horsepower not on the number of nipples, as in England. And on the wall of the garage was a large notice reading: 'All mechanical repairs bear a labour charge of 12 francs per hour and all electrical repairs are charged at 15 francs per hour'. This idea might well be followed over here. Great interest was displayed in our Vauxhall, many of its features being quite unknown in France...'

Motoring was moving toward a new age. Cars like the Big Six sported a self-lubricating chassis and a firm called Wefco were offering spring covers that kept the grease in and the wet and dirt out. These Wefco gaiters completely sealed the spring, giving 100 per cent protection. A complete set 'could be fitted in ten minutes and taken off in even less time'.

All these vehicle improvements called for an ever increasing array of raw materials, some unimaginable. In his 1935 article *What Flannel Means to You*, W.J. Seymour was not offering an education for con men. He was referring to a recent factory visit:

Oil filters being made in 1937, at AC's Dunstable factory. The girl has sewn a piece of flannel in such a way that it resembles a cricket pad. (Vauxhall Motors)

'I went out to the new A.C. Factory at Dunstable, and one of the first things I saw when I got inside... was a row of girls working sewing machines. they were surrounded by millions of yards (it seemed like that anyway) of flannel. Now AC make (among other things) sparking plugs, speedometers, fuel pump gauges of various kinds, and oil filters. I wondered which of these the flannel was for. Answer – the oil filters. Girls take oblong of flannel, double it long ways, sews it into a flannel bag, with a number of seams to create channels like a cricket pad. Strong metal containers are made with two holes in the bottom, one with a brass union and a similar union in the corner of the flannel bag which is rolled very tightly and given a gauze metal shield before being forced into the container with the brass union sticking out of the second hole, creating a way in and out for the oil.'

Oil filters were necessary because carbon particles and bits of road grit and metal mixes with the oil as it lubricates the hot running engine. Circulated oil oozed through the gauze before getting back into the engine's lubrication system. research showed that nothing larger than .00005in in diameter could get through the fabric of the flannel.' This kind of detail about the design and manufacture of

The road sign warns 'impractical for motor cars' in this mid-1930s scene, but this latest model Light
Six can cope. (Vauxhall Motors)

just one component enlightens us as to why the motor industry was already such
a large scale source of employment.

In the mid-1930s, *Vauxhall Motorist* proudly ran a series on their car-making
stalwarts. Among them was Jack Hart, a special grade setter in the gear machine
shop:

'Under his care come the machines that a make for a quick and efficient change whenever
you use the gear lever. Since he has been doing that job for twenty three of the twenty five
years he has been with the firm, it is a safe assumption that every reader is using a gear that
Jack Hart helped produce. When a gear blank arrives, it is just a forging; to the untutored eye
it looks rather like a discoloured lump of clay... it is not just a case of putting metal in one
end of a machine and waiting for the gear to drop out of the other; at each stage of its career
it is checked and measured, measured and checked before continuing to its next stage of
development... Many years ago Jack Hart went in search of gold in the Klondyke: and what's
more he found gold. How much has not been told, but for some reason he forsook the life
and returned to his old work. Perhaps, as many have often suspected, gold-digging is not all
it is made out to be. Or perhaps a gold mine is much the same as any other manufacturing
concern, only further removed from the benefits of civilisation. Anyway, he returned richer

in experience, if not in pocket, and it is the benefit of that experience that he gives not only to his work mates in the section, but also in his capacity as an elected member of our Management Advisory Committee and of the Welfare Council. He has long been a vice president of our Benevolent Fund, of which he was an instigator.'

There could be no doubt that GM was analogous to a gold mine, with many dependent on its workings. The memoirs of Alfred P. Sloan depicted the tremendous might of General Motors, established by the expansion programme of 1925-29. He wrote of the period:

'We expanded our merchandising operations including overseas assembly plants and warehouses and so brought our products closer to the ultimate consumer... Total assets increased from $704 million to $1.3 billion. Unit car and truck sales from $1.2 million in 1926 to $1.9 million in 1929.'

Through the 1930s, GMC spent $346 million on new plant and equipment.

GMC's research laboratories were of vital importance to the growing empire. Motor vehicles had advanced little by 1920, but better roads eased the ride. Sliding gear shifts, unbalanced engines and two wheel brakes were just part of the awkward business of driving. Gear ratios had to be improved and the problem of knock eliminated – vibration caused by the explosion of fuel gas in each firing cylinder. An ingredient needed adding to the fuel to absorb this energy and so smooth the engine running. At first engineers thought they could solve the problem by advancing or retarding the ignition, but experiments revealed fuel knock was the bigger factor. Charles Kettering of GM research put tetraethyl lead in the petrol, then benzol was added. GMC formed the Ethyl Gasoline Corporation, experimenting with anti-knock qualities of fuels, measuring them according to Dr Graham Edgar's octane scale. In 1926 Kettering developed a single-cylinder, variable compression, test engine to test different fuels. As well as establishing the right amounts of anti-knock factor, engines were re-designed to absorb shock waves. Crankshaft vibration was reduced and the search for better gear changing led to the first research on automatic transmissions.

By 1934 GM had developed the hydramatic step ratio gearbox which shifted automatically under torque, using a fluid coupling within the transmission. GMC formed the Detroit Transmission Division and the hydramatic gearbox was first fitted to the 1940 Oldsmobile and the 1941 Cadillac. The organisation was also working on a similar system for trucks and coaches. The principle was simple enough, rather like an electric powered fan being positioned next to a freewheeling fan. As the powered fan turns, the draught spins the free fan which starts turning. In the motor vehicle, the powered fan is the engine flywheel, the draught is an oil spray and the free fan is the clutch plate connected to the road wheels. Additional wheels were necessary to change the fluid flow characteristics, thus affecting the difference in speeds between engine and drive shaft. With war approaching, GM were asked to develop the system for tanks.

The Vauxhall Motor Company were not immediate beneficiaries of all this research, and the development of their motor cars would soon be suspended by the start of war. In the early stages of acquisition, GM had wondered whether to write off the Vauxhall acquisition as a bad investment, since they already owned the successful Opel Company in Germany.

As an established quality car dealer, Vauxhall had a fraction of Austin's dealerships and there was uncertainty as to the best course for Vauxhall to take. The only certainty seemed to be in the market for small trucks and coaches. The 1930s were not ideal for exports, but Britain had its colonies. During the 1930s, truck and coach sales exceeded cars in most years, around half going abroad. With competitors like AEC and Leyland concentrating on heavy trucks, the field was open to Bedford and its strong lightweights. Africa, Australia and New Zealand were easy markets for vehicles exported in kit form. A major order was also obtained from Afghanistan in 1937. A 'Motoring News' report in *The People* (11 November 1937) reported:

'British firm bags Record Truck Order. A British-built truck has won the biggest overseas lorry contract ever signed because of its sturdy construction and speed. Yesterday the Vauxhall firm received an order for 350 three ton trucks from the Afghanistan Government. Recently tests were carried out over a twenty-two mile course against other makes in the wildest districts of Afghanistan – a Bedford truck fully loaded climbed mountain passes, crossed river beds, tore along tracks in half the time it took a foreign-built truck that was also being tested.'

The order was increased to 488 and testament to the versatile and rugged lorries that Vauxhall were building under the Bedford marque. The Afganistan government were working to promote their country as a major cotton producer. Though they had no manufacturing facilities they aimed to export their entire cotton crop, which is where the Bedford trucks came into the picture. Most of Afghanistan's cotton was being grown at Mazr-I-Shariff (over 500 miles of mountain passes and primitive roads from Peshawar on the Indian side of the Khyber Pass) where it was despatched by rail to the port of Karachi for shipment to customers.

Without railways, Afghanistan's only transport solution was by truck. They estimated a need for around 400 vehicles and staged trials to find the most suitable make. All were examined and subjected to gruelling tests before the Bedford was chosen. Bedford and its nearest competitor were tested while carrying equal loads. The Bedford completed the journey in half the time of its rival. The authorities were so impressed that they increased the initial order from 350 to 488. The vehicles were fitted with special drop sides. It was the country's largest truck order at the time.

As mid-1930s advertising pointed out:

'Everywhere you go you see these Bedford vans and trucks speeding along roads and earning profits for their owners. For *reliability* is the keynote of Bedford. Day in and

Two doughty little Bedfords working in a 1930s coal yard, an era still in some not inconsiderable part a steam age. (Vauxhall Motors)

day out, in fair weather and foul and with many different loads they speed up delivery schedules and keep down costs per ton mile. Rugged engineering and advanced engineering have made this speedy and economical running possible. Nationwide service facilities and the design and research of Bedfords of the famous Vauxhall factory at Luton are among many other reasons for amazing popularity. Look over the Bedford range at your local Bedford dealer or write direct to Vauxhall Motors Ltd, Edgware Road, N.W.9.'

At that time the 30cwt Bedford chassis cost £175, the drop-side lorry with tilt £217, a 3 way hydraulic tipper £268, ambulance £385, furniture pantechnicon £313, farmer's wagon £291 and a 20-seater Sun Saloon coach £555.

Whilst Bedford were cornering the market for the smaller independent bus and truck operators, two major bus groupings were heading towards the formation of a national bus company, standardising on either Bristol or AEC chassis. The latter were also becoming a dominant influence in the heavy truck field. Nevertheless, the future of Bedford was very sound during the second half of the 1930s. Vauxhall Motors approach to the car market, however, was bound for a significant shift of emphasis. As Alfred P. Sloan concluded in his memoirs:

'Each new generation must meet changes in the automotive market, in the general administration of the enterprises, and in the involvement of the corporation in a changing world. for the present management, the work is only beginning. Some of the problems are similar to those I met in my time, some are problems I never dreamed of. The work of creating goes on.'

Those comments, written in 1962, were just as true nearly thirty years earlier and remain so.

Vauxhall creativity in 1937 came in the shape of the Vauxhall 10/4, H type. *Motor* magazine welcomed its appearance with the comments:

'This is an extraordinary car... it seats four in comfort... exceeds 42 miles per gallon and cannot fail to become one of the most popular cars on the British market.'

The company spent over £1 million on new buildings, machinery and equipment to produce the new model which appeared at the Earls Court Motor Show that October. The Vauxhall Ten featured independent front wheel and constantly varying suspension, hydraulic brakes, all in one steel body and chassis (the first British car of unitary construction), Vauxhall Six Phase carburation, and Vauxhall-controlled synchromesh on second and third gears, body conformity seating. The de luxe version, with no draught ventilation and polychromatic cellulose paint work, cost £182 – £14 more than the standard version. With a 7ft 10in wheelbase, it was the most compact Vauxhall yet, an ideal fit for suburban garages. The car also had to conform with the year-old anti-dazzle rules. Because of increasing traffic speeds and volume, it was illegal to equip a vehicle with non-dippable headlights and old ones had to be modified. Vauxhall H-type performance figures were impressive:

Through the Gears.
0–30 8.0 seconds
0–50 22.5 seconds

On Second Gear
10–30mph 10.5 secs
10–50mph 26.0 seconds
30–50mph 15.5 seconds

The integrated body was a turning point. Open tourers had gradually gone from fashion, saloons being more practical. The whole body shell accelerated production lines. For many years sheet metal had been cut with shears and shaped by hand-held tools. Now the age of huge presses had arrived, shaping the panels to cloth the framework of chassis or body. On the larger car front, customers could purchase the 25hp G type, capable of a staggering 80mph with all the usual features, plus a built-in heater, fog and reversing lights and hydraulic brakes. The standard saloon cost £315, but being built on the old separate chassis system offered a range of alternatives. Even big cars were using less petrol per mile as efficiency was increased, but the driver's role in economy was crucial.

The H type's body shell, showing more clearly the integral structure of the new design. (Vauxhall Motors)

As Maurice Platt observed in his role as technical editor of the *Motor* magazine in 1937,

'A motor car engine exists upon a diet of petrol and air. Its health and energy depend upon three things, the balancing of the diet (which is simply a matter of providing petrol and air in the correct ratio) the thorough mixture of these ingredients and thirdly their delivery through piping arranged to give each cylinder an equal share in quality and quantity of the meal. Properly treated in this way, an engine can make efficient use of the chemical energy in the fuel (by its internal combustion with oxygen).'

Without doubt, the Ten Four represented the way forward, with heavyweight volume luxury motoring almost exclusively the domain of Rolls-Royce and Bentley in British markets. Over 10,000 were sold in the first five months of production and the 12hp model was released in late 1938.

The development of British motor cars had reached a milestone just before another world war stopped production again, and was well summarised by the distinguished and eccentric Professor Low, whose many achievements included demonstrating television in 1914 and a publication called '*The Tendencies of Modern Science*'. Writing in the August 1938 edition of *Vauxhall Motorist*, he penned:

'Broadly speaking, all cars are reasonably good. I think there is hardly any modern chassis of modest horsepower that will not take people along a straight road at 60mph and

It is surprising what a difference another seven inches on the wheel base of the H type made, converting it into the roomier I type, Twelve Four. Fitted with a 1442 cc OHV engine, the car managed 35mpg. The young lady sets this model off a treat. (Vauxhall Motors)

achieve 26mph average, with a petrol consumption of something in the neighbourhood of 20mpg. Not to beat about the bush, the experienced driver takes it for granted that normal reliability and pace must exist in any car worthy of the name. And he realises that the difference between a good and bad machine is measurable, not by the work it does, but by the fuss it makes and by the manner in which that work is carried out. My own opinion is that there are very few cars in the entire world which really makes motoring a pleasure... and can only be made available to the motoring public in one of two ways:

a) the purchaser must be asked to spend a lot of money or b) the designers must be first class men.

'In the Vauxhall 25 I tested (and in all the other Vauxhalls) these problems have been overcome in the most sensible way.'

Far greater problems were around the corner and not so easily overcome. The Luton showrooms were boarded up and blacked out as the grim reality of the conflict ahead dawned on the local population, but the challenges of the Second World War would accelerate vehicle technology into a new age of speed, comfort and style.

CHAPTER FIVE

A CHANGING WORLD

Luton's population at the start of the twentieth century was already large at 36,400 and by the end of the Second World War it exceeded 100,000. War also transformed General Motors from the world's largest car maker into the largest supplier of war materials – providing 77 per cent of the Corporation's net income between 1940 and 1944. War transformed the nation, changing attitudes and stimulating technological advance. Bedford truck designs became the basis for a new breed of army vehicles, the QL making history as the company's first 4x4. The Luton factory was also involved with building the Churchill tank. Appeasers in Government and across the nation ensured the country was unready for war. Among other inadequacies, Britain had under 100 tanks. Vauxhall performed the remarkable feat of designing and building a new one, ready for production within the year. Owen Hardisty recalled joining the company as a fourteen year old in the early days of war:

'I remember when I started, Jack Hardy was a tool maker in X block, I was in there with him, it was August 1940, when they bombed X block and the roof came off. Seven were killed in there, along with another thirty-seven elsewhere at the plant. I'd spoken to Dennis Orchard ten minutes before he died. They were working on the early jet engines in V block. The Churchill tank was 38 tons, but useless because it had a pea shooter for a turret gun, with a three inch Howitzer in the hull. It was improved when they built a 40-ton version with a new turret.'

Men were called up, labour was in short supply, there were worsening industrial relations and women were to the fore on the home front. Owen said:

'I remember women working on the tank engines. I was just a dogsbody running errands when I started my apprenticeship. I remember Monty Johnson, a brilliant engineer. Hayward Tylers machined the turret rings and Newton Chambers the castings and caterpillar tracks. When I joined on April 17th 1940, I was paid 12s 6d a week, plus 2s war bonus. Mr Simpson was the Chief Engineer and everything was hushed outside his office door, only the ticking of the clock and the typewriters would be heard . There was a very thick carpet outside Mr Bartlett's office. I was sent there with about £25 to cash a cheque when they were going

The Churchill Tank MKI receives some finishing touches in the Vauxhall Bedford works. (Vauxhall Motors)

Mr Winston Churchill (not yet Sir) inspects his namesake tank on the proving grounds around Luton, along with army top brass. (Vauxhall Motors)

Young Owen Hardisty at the time he joined the Vauxhall Bedford Motor Company. (Vauxhall Motors)

up to the Midlands to solve an off-site problem. The cashier's department was in F block. There was a walkway around the top and you looked down into a stairwell. The thing that struck me about Vauxhall was that the appearance of class was less obvious than elsewhere. Because it was an American firm even underlings would address the boss by his first name. Some production workers would address Reg. Pearson as Reg. because he had started on the shop floor.'

Frank Ford's father had been secretary to the managing director in the late 1920s. Frank said:

'My father didn't have a clue what went on under the bonnet, but his working for Vauxhall kindled my interest. I didn't see much of the cars when I was a young boy, production was low and father didn't talk much about work. We had to move to Kimpton Road when our house was demolished to make way for P block. In 1941, I took a five year apprenticeship, learning all the trappings of engineering.'

Capturing beach heads and bringing equipment ashore is a major wartime challenge. One idea had been to modify a Bedford QL, nicknamed the Giraffe, to travel from landing craft across shallow water. It did not work and so this more successful 'waterproofing' approach was adopted – seen here on trial in Wardown Park, Luton. (Vauxhall Motors)

Luckily, Frank missed the worst of the Luftwaffe's attentions in 1940, but Vauxhall were still heavily involved in the war effort. Frank recalled:

'They built the tanks in a part of the factory that it was hard to get them out of because the driver's view was obstructed by pillars. We built four varieties of army trucks as well. The QL was four-wheel-drive and a convoy of these was not to be forgotten. Those transmission boxes howled. We called them square faces. They were a bit macho. A tough vehicle for a tough job. the army swore by them.'

Tanks, like the army lorries, were tested in Wardown Park.

The British paid a high price for US wartime assistance, including having to wind down its Empire. In February 1943, Alfred P. Sloan received a letter from Edward Riley, General Motors' vice-president and general manager of overseas operations, providing a summary of the political and economic situation in the post-war world, assuming that the United States would hold a stronger position. Riley wrote:

Bomb damage at the Luton Bedford Plant in 1940. (Vauxhall Motors)

'Another discernible trend in England is the undoubted growing realisation that the future well-being and safety of the British Commonwealth can best be protected by closer political collaboration with the United States.

General Motors' other European operation was more problematic during hostilities. In 1942 the entire investment of $35 million in Opel was written off as Opel supported the German war effort. In 1945 Russia failed in a bid to take Opel as part reparations and by 1949 the company was replenishing GM profits with car and truck sales up to 40,000.

Vauxhall more than made up for the enslavement of its German sister plant, producing 5,640 Churchill tanks, 4 million rocket engine components, 750,000 helmets, thousands of 6-pounder armour-piercing shells and the sides of over 5 million jerry cans. The factory also produced decoy trucks and aircraft as well as being associated with aircraft development and production, mainly at the neighbouring local airfield where de Havilland Mosquito bombers were built. Vauxhall did 95 per cent of the work on the first twelve jet propulsion engines ever built, in conditions of extreme secrecy. They also made over 4 million venturi tubes, part of the rocket projectile and during one emergency period turned out 6-pounder armour-piercing shot at the rate of 5,000 a week. When helmets were scarce, the works rushed out 3 million. Body engineers also designed a mounting

A RATHER UNUSUAL ASPECT OF VEHICLE DESIGN
WAS THE DEVELOPEMENT OF THIS 'MW' INFLATABLE TRUCK

Making inflatable decoy army lorries, like this one, were among many other of the Vauxhall Bedford's other wartime activities. (Vauxhall Motors)

for a 20mm quick-firing gun and truck engineers designed a resilient wheel which was not needed but would have been if the rubber situation had worsened. The sheet metal department spent 80 per cent of its wartime 'tooling up' for other firms; making jigs, dies and fixtures for speedier production. They made dies for the Hercules engine cylinder barrel at the rate of three a fortnight and work on mines, torpedoes, radio location and bombs among other things. Vauxhall also provided a team of liaison workers to instruct service personnel in the operation of W.D. Bedfords and tanks.

Vauxhall became expert in the art of camouflage, the entire works being painted to blend in with the neighbouring hills as Luton continued to be a target for the enemy throughout the war. The plant was lucky to escape as lighty as it did. In the closing stages of the war a V2 rocket, travelling at nearly three times the speed of sound, hit the Commer Karrier despatch shop in Biscot Road and even Whipsnade Zoo was hit.

Wartime work was long and hard. The normal hours of working were 46½ hours per week for hourly paid employees (47 hours on the night shift)and factory staff, and 40½ hours for office staff. As a wartime measure, Vauxhall operated four staggered day shifts which meant workers could be required to come in at 7.30 a.m., 8 a.m., 8.30 a.m. or 9 a.m., depending on the shift on which their Shop or

With so many men away at the front, young ladies like this one had to take on some of the heavy work on the home front. This lady is involved in the building of Bedford trucks. (Vauxhall Motors)

Division was working. There was an hour for lunch, half hour for tea and two ten-minute rest breaks with tea available from trolleys around the factory, at one penny a cup. Workers could be called upon to do overtime, including working through statutory holidays. Good labour relations were essential but difficult under such trying conditions. The company issued a statement on 21 May 1942:

'The Management of this Company recognises only too well, and appreciates equally strongly, the great work that trade Unions have done, and are still doing for the good of working folks, a subject in which we in this Company are keenly and strongly interested as our general policies show. And we will help Trade Unions in this work (as we have done)to the fullest extent of our power, even leading the way for them sometimes, when new ground has to be broken.

'What we do not do is make any distinction between one person and another, that is, between a Union member or a non Union man. We have a responsibility to all: and the question of membership of any organisation must be a matter for a man's own free decision in a free country ...we must treat all our employees alike, be they union or non union...'

Women also worked as army drivers. This member of WAAC is about to deliver the 200,000th wartime Bedford, a QL. All three services used the tough Bedford four-wheel drive trucks. (Vauxhall Motors)

Twenty-six employees were elected to the Management Advisory Committee, a permanent round table conference aiming to achieve the highest level of co-operation between workers and management. Benevolent, group insurance and welfare schemes also promoted an atmosphere of care for the workforce. Loss of experienced men to the war also placed a premium on schemes to develop the skills of boys between fourteen and sixteen, taken on as office boys with a view to developing their potential at the local Technical College and then on to Vauxhall apprenticeship schemes.

Of course management realised the value of sound trade unionism in helping to manage grievances according to set procedure and elaborated a process with the AEU, sating that:

'The Management concerned expresses its complete willingness at all times to see any union official or interested in such matters, or interested in any other matters that concern the well being and progress of the Company and its employees.'

Health and safety was not quite the industry that it is today but in a large car plant was never stinted on, the site being replete with nursing staff, surgeries and welfare workers. With so many wartime women workers, safety needed a special approach. In a wartime booklet issued by the Personnel and Welfare Department, the advice was:

'Safety is particularly important in the case of women workers where the dictates of fashion provide an overwhelming urge to change the style of shoes, dress, hair styles, and the like, every few months! Unfortunately fashions are not always designed with a view to accident prevention during the process of earning one's living.

'The Women's Welfare Supervisor and Assistants in each factory area, therefore devote much time to safety clothing in all its details, and here is a outline of the facilities available.

'Boiler Suits.
1) It is a condition of employment that all women working on factory jobs previously performed by men, and all other work specified by the Women's Welfare Supervisor, wear women's boiler suits. the 'rule' is obviously made in the employee's own interest.
2) Each woman worker is provided with a set of three numbered suits of correct size, which only she is entitled to wear.
3) These boiler suits remain the property of the Company who accept responsibility for cleaning, repairing, and replacements.
4) Wearers are asked to all reasonable care against unnecessary damage or loss.
5) Suits must be handed in on termination of employment.

'Inspection Coats
1) All women working on Inspection work are asked to wear inspection coats or overalls provided. Inspection employees are entitled to two coats or overalls provided. Inspection employees are entitled to two coats or overalls in twelve months, but to help offset laundry difficulties they may, if they prefer, be issued with three- at one time- to cover eighteen months' wear.
2) Wearers are asked to accept responsibility for laundering and repair and to wear a clean overall each week.

'Coupons
Under present Board of Trade regulations it is stipulated that wearers must surrender coupons for boiler suits, coats and overalls. A set of boiler suits 'costs' 12 coupons, coats and overalls 3 coupons. Women are asked to give up 4 coupons on starting work, while the balance is collected over the next twelve months.

'Safety Caps, Shoes and clogs
These are necessary on all work involving the use of machinery.
The whole idea of Safety Caps is to cover the hair completely as a protection against stray wisps and ends becoming involved in machinery...'

Mercifully it was not all work in those dark wartime years. The company had always been keen to promote recreation, providing what they called a democratic Recreation Club run by a General Council comprising representatives from each of ten Works Groups together with chairmen of the various sporting and recreational sections and two representatives appointed by the company. The council also ran the canteen, which had its own pig-fattening unit, and licensed bar, handling a budget of over £100,000 per year.

Britain was badly prepared for war, the population having endured mass unemployment, poor health and education and a succession of inept governments. The nation could easily have been defeated by Nazi Germany and US support came in the nick of time. When the conflict ended Britain was nearly bankrupt and the United States not well disposed toward helping the rebirth of the old Empire.

GMC executives from the US arrived in Luton to show the way along with David Jones, the firm's longest serving design executive. Sir John Anderson, Chancellor in 1944, favoured small step car taxation at £1 per 100cc. Hugh Dalton introduced this after the 1945 election, but it forced the industry into a multiplicity of models affecting economies of scale. A simpler solution would have been pay as you go with petrol tax. S.C. Butler, assistant managing director of Vauxhall wrote in the *Vauxhall Motorist* (April 1946)

'Why were British manufacturers denied their chance to remove the slur that American navvies often ride to work in better cars than do Britain's skilled craftsmen?'

The answer seemed to be administrative simplicity in car taxation but high mileage customers objected.

With cars in short supply, customer relations were not easy. Pre-war had been an age of variety of models to suit the complicated tax system. Vauxhall needed to concentrate resources to win the export battle. In December 1946, the *Vauxhall Motorist* published the comments:

'...we must get motor cars more freely owned amongst work people of our country, and get away from the idea that in the modern world a motor car is essentially a luxury product. Towards this end we feel that some simplification of our tax structures would be a very important first step.'

Pre-war Britain had one car per every twenty five people compared to one for every five in the United States. GMC could see much potential for their British subsidiary, but though wages were half the US rate and Vauxhall labour supportive, UK materials were comparatively very expensive.

In 1946 Vauxhall announced that they would concentrate on producing two body styles instead of three. Simplification allowed price reduction and production economies, helping to meet the pent up demand for cars whilst maintaining quality. In mid-1947 the Government abolished the horsepower-related taxation system in favour of a flat rate, allowing Vauxhall to replace the 10hp engine with a 12hp four-cylinder block and a new 2.25 litre six-cylinder unit. The new rate applied from 1 January 1948.

Six phase carburation was a key innovation, combining the greatest fuel economy with best possible engine efficiency and petrol economy. With careful driving, 12hp models gave 35mpg and 14hp gave 30mpg. The L type emerged in 1948 as either Wyvern or Velox models. The former had received the H type 12hp engine and the latter the six-cylinder. Both had the revolutionary rear-hinged bonnet replacing the split bonnet. Though there was some style continuity with the H type, the new model showed strong elements of the US flair that would be the shape of things soon to come and during 1945-47 £36 million would be spent on doubling car production, excavating over 1.5 million tons of chalk and clay from the Chilterns to accommodate the 1 million square feet of building. The spoil was used to extend neighbouring Luton Airport by 12 acres and to reclaim 32 acres of Luton Hoo Park. Steel work came from the US, having been intended for a wartime GMC plant making B-29 bombers. The new AA block was among the largest steel frame structures of the day. Total net sales for 1946 were £19,839,667, and pre-tax profits £3,852,317 – representing 4.3 per cent of turnover. Costs were rising, new equipment was needed while trade associations were doing their bests to protect existing job structures when modernisation was needed.

Vauxhall resumed publication of their *Vauxhall Motorist* magazine with Number 1 of Volume 7 in April 1946. Opening editorial was apologetic:

> 'we were not scheduled as a car-producing factory: The authorities had other plans for us, with the result that between the end of 1939 and the beginning of 1946 we made barely a hundred or so Vauxhall cars. There were quite a lot of them used by the services (particularly the Navy and RAF) but they were mostly impressed when the war started either from our factory – those that were already in the "system" being taken over as we made them – or from private owners. Of course we made Bedfords. scores of thousands of them for the forces. In addition to the familiar "square face" WD type, we designed and produced many thousands of a model known as the "QL". This the army called a 4X4, which meant that it could be used with power on the back wheels only, or on all four wheels...'

Bedford vehicles were built for many specialist roles, such as ammunition transport, ambulances, dental surgeries, radio vehicles, command trucks, smoke throwers, offices, workshops, armoured vehicles and gun tractors to name a few. All had to be rugged and the war taught Vauxhall/Bedford how to test.

Vauxhall Motorist added:

> 'To those who imagined that post-war motoring would become a matter of streamlined super cars, rocket propelled and silent, achieving 100mph, maybe 200mph or even more – and of course crash proof – post-war motoring is going to be a trifle disappointing. Cars are still cars much as we knew them before the war and, for that matter, as we knew them during the war. And so Vauxhalls remain Vauxhalls and all that the name stands for.'

Good Labour relations were essential. Vauxhall believed that steady policy of keeping the people in the company well-informed, talking to them about

"*After what I saw 'out there'*
no other tyre
will really satisfy me now"

Firestone
BEST TODAY ★ STILL BETTER TOMORROW

The Second World War, though traumatic for millions, forced the pace of technological advance. This evocative advert from 1946 shows a service man speaking in the language of contemporary film heroes, his subject the need and availability of safer tyres. (Vauxhall Motors)

company problems, achievements, doubts, and difficulties had developed a balance and understanding which was invaluable. By December 1946 there were 11,588 employed on the Luton site. Vauxhall was a popular employer. The social facilities, management advisory committee (introduced by managing director Sir Charles Bartlett), employee benefit scheme, group health and life insurance, and training programmes made all feel part of the team. The re-training centre for men who had suffered war injury or mishaps at work was another valuable sign that Vauxhall cared for its staff. Sir Charles Bartlett also introduced the father and son system of recruitment, a system known as the Vauxhall family, and a profit-sharing scheme.

The Labour Government elected by a landslide in 1945 was committed to full employment and a planned economy. War had left capital equipment run down, reduced housing stock, exhausted workers and massive balance of payments problems. It was committed to extensive nationalisation of basic industries, social welfare, full employment and a planned economy. These targets were all very well but there was too little money. By 1947, a coal shortage and the worst winter since 1880 made matters appear even more hopeless. An export drive was essential, this would mean even worse shortages for the indigenous population, but it focused the minds of those directing Vauxhall Motors. Until 1948, the company relied on the pre-war H, I, and J types, most going abroad.

"The Story of Vauxhall"

1857—1946

A souvenir book published to commemorate the jubilee of the motor industry and Vauxhall's own 89th birthday as manufacturers, firstly, of marine engines and, for the last 43 years, of motor vehicles. There are many interesting illustrations of early Vauxhalls including, of course, the famous record breakers.

PRICE 3/6 POST FREE

Available from—
Public Relations Dept., Vauxhall
Motors Ltd., Luton, Beds.

A trio of adverts from the 1946 world of motoring adds a little more seasoning to the tale. (Vauxhall Motors)

Car production lines had been dismantled during the war and with a big steel shortage, getting the lines re-started was challenging. There was a desperate hunger for transport. The Labour Government saw a nationalised, integrated haulage and rail service as a large part of the solution, eliminating waste. Vauxhall limited their expectations to 60,000 units for 1947, following unit sales of 53,586 in 1946. Of the latter figure, 19,722 were cars and 33,864 commercials – 22,867 units, equal to 42.7 per cent, were exported. Most exports went to Australia, New Zealand, South Africa, Denmark, India and Argentina. The Government's 'Economic Survey for 1947 argued: that failing to develop the export trade 'in the next two or three years so that we can afford to buy enough imports would mean continued food rationing, much less smoking and private motoring.' The Government neglected to point out how much it was spending abroad clinging to the notion that Britain was still a world power. The price of this posturing was very little freedom from grim toil for the majority in Britain, freedom was still a dream.

'And since in this brave new world we all want freedom from something, Vauxhall motoring can offer us freedom from rattles', wrote the editor of *Vauxhall Motorist* in April 1946. He went on to explain that this was achieved by integral design, the whole car body being made into one piece from welded sections. This was technology akin to an aircraft's stressed skin, the whole car being engineered as a car, not as a chassis or afterthought, being built up of steel pressings welded together. This may have been the age of austerity, but Vauxhalls were fitted with

On a late 1940s open country road, we see some old style courtesy as the driver of an I type Vauxhall is waved on by the trusty Bedford O truck driver. It would be a while before new models hit the roads from Vauxhalls who were busy extending and re-equipping their facilities after war work. (Vauxhall Motors)

a number of extras, such as an ashtray recessed in the centre of the back of the front seat, an electric clock run off the battery and 'no draught' ventilation, sun visor, self cancelling traffic indicators, two sun visors, twin mechanical and almost silent windscreen wipers.

Those wipers were needed during the terrible winter of 1947, as was anti-freeze. With spring came *Vauxhall Motorist's* reminder that 'anti-freeze has a peculiar tendency to loosen dirt on the walls of water passages, urging a purge to flush it out'. The editor wrote:

'All right, so motor cars look different now. Instead of being high, wide and anything but handsome, they are low, sleek and graceful. Ungainliness has become near beauty and even a ten-year-old seems strange in appearance compared with the models of today... the chief reason for a car's changing appearance is fairly obvious. We live – as if anyone didn't know it – in a changing world. the trend is always towards simplicity and ease of handling in design of all everyday things, from a motor bus to a tooth brush...'

For all the changes Vauxhall still considered leather the best material for upholstery, being durable, moisture resistant and easy to clean.

The editor added that now reliability could be taken for granted, 'it is the good looking car that sells.' To this end the styling division at the Luton factory was crucial. Hidden away in the engineering department, not because it was so small, but because most of its work took place behind locked doors, the men of Vauxhall were working on the cars of the future, guarding their secrets as jealously as any dress designer.

Brilliant ideas took time to fruit in those austere times. Vauxhall's PR manager wrote:

'it should be the aim of all of us in the motor industry to cut down as much as possible, the amount of "looking after" which a car needs... in 1896 when motoring began... instruction books were highly technical; one almost had to be an engineer to understand them. That was right and proper because one almost had to be an engineer to drive the darn cars anyway... this technical tradition persisted... until 1936 when we introduced the simply written, well illustrated 'magaziney' type of instruction book which has since become so popular. Now we are wondering about starting another revolution. During the war, we have learnt a lot about vehicle maintenance. An awful lot... We turned out something like 250,000 Bedford truck... (we had representatives, "civilians in battle dress" in every theatre of war.). Services like RASA used the method of "16 daily tasks stem to stern, vehicle always under examination". The army system is extreme, but our instruction books can build on this. Suppose we could work out about eight separate jobs and asked you to do one every Saturday afternoon say. Would you be interested? You would, of course, choose your own day, but in our new type of instruction book we would publish a list of dates covering each week for several years and give full details of what should be done during every week throughout that period.'

In September 1946, Mr Wilberforce asked *Vauxhall Motorist* whether it was worth him travelling the extra mile to his Vauxhall dealer for service rather than the nearest garage. They replied:

A smart I type being admired by the ladies at a country cottage. For some years after the war, Britain remained superficially unchanged, motoring still mainly the preserve of the upper and middle class, the models stately and the womenfolk rather haughty. (Vauxhall Motors)

'...a Vauxhall dealer knows Vauxhalls and every nut and bolt on the car. He is to a Vauxhall what a good doctor is to his long standing patient... he knows them so well he can usually see that they don't have much chance of going wrong at all.'

With cars still in short supply, this was good advice from Vauxhall. Pre-war cars were going to be a common sight for years to come as Britain began a very slow recovery. Getting production up to demand was hampered by material shortages. There were 11,588 working at the Luton plant by December 1946, with big increases on the technical side Vauxhall needed two pounds of coal to make one unit of power when total requirements were for 800,000 units a week. In 1947 their gas producing plant made 19,000,000 cubic feet of gas per week. Delays to restoring rubber supplies from Malaya meant prolonged use of synthetic rubber, always a poor substitute, being prone to blow outs, making braking and accelerating more difficult, leading to higher fuel consumption. Vauxhall engineers calculated a 2.2mpg difference at 30mph.

It was a cruel irony that a population that had given so much toward a free world had to see the fruits of its labour being exported to pay for reconstruction and a dubious foreign policy. During the Labour Government, 1945-50, national output rose three times faster than consumption was allowed to, at 30 per cent. The resulting shortage of cars encouraged a black market, making it possible for a new car to be bought, registered and driven a few miles before being sold for much more than the list price plus purchase tax. Amongst many examples was a 14hp Vauxhall bought for £480 and resold for £1,000. Those in the know could make fortunes, not surprisingly when there was as much as a two-year waiting list for a new car. This led the Motor Association to enforce covenants preventing buyers from selling their new cars until they were at least six months old. Meanwhile Vauxhall staff made do with pre-war models that had clocked around 100,000 miles each as 50 per cent of production went overseas.

For all the shortages, Britain had plenty of traffic. By 1939 there were 14.5 motor vehicles for every mile of road (excluding motorcycles) compared to only 9.7 in the United States. Early post-war estimates expected 12 million cars by 1963 and the Ministry of Transport said that 1951-56 'will be dedicated to comprehensive reconstruction of the principal national routes.'

Summer road congestion was also affected by a decline in foreign travel. In 1939, five Britons went abroad for every foreigner who visited Britain. In the late 1940s most natives had no chance to of going abroad. British resorts were consequently crowded, miserable and expensive. *Vauxhall Motorist* was still concerned that so many were pre-war:

'...It seems to be a fair assumption that the condition of some of the cars now being driven is not really good enough for them to be used on roads that are not only crowded to almost 1939 levels, but are often a long way below 1939 standards of quality...'

But the reporter felt there were exceptions:

'Old though they may be, some of these Vauxhalls... the last eight years have proved again and again that if a Vauxhall is well and regularly maintained, it can go on being safe and enjoyable to drive long after its owner thought it impossible... Service for Safety.

If a person could not afford motoring during those hard times, Vauxhall gave comprehensive advice on how best to lay up the car. Their magazine even included a piece called 'Going My Way', by Frank Illingworth, explaining how:

'Hitch hiking provides a particular branch of comradeship not to be found in the ordinary way of travelling.'

In 1947, traffic volume reached a post-war peak in 1947, with a record for new registrations – the new flat rate tax of £10 per annum was helped boost demand The Government also managed a claw back by imposing double purchase tax on cars costing over £1,000. Tax revenue on cars was running at £100,000,000 per annum. However, the changes were good for Vauxhall who could focus on larger, better-proportioned and cheaper engines now that the draughtsman was not guided by the tax disc! Thus *Vauxhall Motorist* reported in August 1947:

'...engines whisper where once they roared. Bodies no longer rattle. And gearboxes, once the noisiest of mechanisms, now produce nothing more than a hum. Chief reason for the quietness of the gearbox on today's Vauxhalls is that they use helical gears in place of spur gears that once were universal. Spur gears have teeth cut straight across, parallel to the shafts that carry them.'

Vauxhall were also pleased to announce that there was no more need to oil rear springs on the latest Vauxhalls as they had plastic interleaving which would be harmed by penetrating oil. They just needed a wipe with Lockheed brake fluid.

New tax laws signalled the end of the Vauxhall Ten in September 1947 – 55,000 'Tens' had been sold from 1945-47. Hardly changed since 1938, it had led the way forward, but now production would concentrate on the 12hp four cylinder and 14hp six-cylinder models. Outstanding orders for the 'Ten' were filled by the 'Twelve' which was cost exactly the same: £422 8s 4d, including purchase tax. The engine was slightly larger and slower revving – 1,845rpm at 30mph compared with 2040rpm. Smoother running, it had a longer life. Engines were also benefiting from detergent oils which had been developed for wartime extremes. Esso superlube could justifiably be sold with the claim that it saved engine wear as oil technology continued to improve. The new Dunlop tyre was wider and lower pressure with stepped tread to improve performance.

The annual report for 1947 was promising, but 26 per cent more cars could have been built but for steel restrictions and other shortages. Exports of 1,000 vehicles were delayed by wheel shortages and there was a need to bring facilities and equipment up to date. Sales figures were 30,376 cars, 31,077 commercial plus and bountiful spares. Car exports numbered 17,872 units and commercials 10,818. The figures represented a 15 per cent improvement on 1946.

Vauxhall could not leave their increasing good fortune dependent on the nation's shambolic infrastructure and so announced the opening of their new diesel generating plant on 30 December 1948. The new plant had an output of 5,000kW, was the largest private plant in Europe and could supply half the factory's electricity needs.

Life seemed to be looking up for the motor industry when, in May 1948, the *Vauxhall Motorist* opined:

'At the time we go to press Mr Gaitskill has not made his eagerly awaited statement on basic petrol, but the feeling is growing that the next month or two will see the return to the road of the pleasure driver... Our bet is that we shall see a return of a gallon a coupon back on May 1st. But by now you know.'

Meanwhile the Minister of Fuel could consider supplementary petrol allowances and police could make tests with paper treated to react to commercial petrol.

Chickens could not be counted too soon. Government policy remained restrictive, a situation exacerbated by borrowing dollars and trying to prop up sterling as a reserve currency. Against this background, comparing Vauxhall's 1947 figures with the average from 1937–39, it was clear that raising prices was no solution and costs had to fall. Lower costs would come from better machinery, equipment and planning. The government's target for the motor industry, in 1948, called for 75 per cent of all cars and 55 per cent of all commercials to be exported.

Meanwhile *Vauxhall Motorist* offered maintenance tips to keep the old car going, using language that seems quaint now but was comforting at the time; a feature on the starter motor observed how it was 'the most neglected – and yet one of the most trouble-free components in the car.' And in case the steadily improving tyres on offer let you down, there was a Vauxhall foot pump that was '…easy to operate, quick in action, lasts a lifetime. The best car pump that money can buy.' Tested and approved by Vauxhall engineers, it cost £2 7s 6d and the 'non-return valve makes every stroke count'. Other useful accessories that year included 'an ashtray for your 10hp or 12hp' for 4 shillings, plus 1s 7½d purchase tax. There was also the
'No Nu Way' car mats, tailored for your Vauxhall (10, 12 & 14hp, post-war models). 'These modern made-to-measure mats look neat and clean always and are guaranteed for 10 years. £3 17s 6d per set plus 18s 11d purchase tax. Your Vauxhall Dealer will be pleased to show you.' For the *pièce de résistance* of the day, a person needed the Vauxhall Echo Car Radio, with 'five fine features; looks good, pre set tuning, splendid performance, excellent reproduction, easy installation – only four holes have to be drilled'. Valves were guaranteed for ninety days and parts for six months. This was all for £22 1s, plus purchase tax. A telescopic aerial was £1 12s 6d extra.

Things were clearly improving all round and in March 1948 Britain's export figures were the highest for twenty-eight years and for Vauxhall they were the highest ever with 5,632 cars and trucks valued at £1,500,000. Sadly, however, there were few signs of improvement to the national infrastructure. Foreign policy, like international debt repayment, was expensive and the integrated transport system floundering. The editor of *Vauxhall Motorist* wrote that:

'Britain at present had possibly the finest system of hard surfaced roads in the world, but has virtually no completed main roads of modern type, and must needs rectify this situation without delay… no responsible authorities appear to have appreciated that a modern community of people must circulate within its own boundaries, not merely for pleasure, but for the efficiency and mental vigour of the nation as a whole…'

He went on to disparage the all-important Watling Street as:

'being in parts little better than a country lane, with raised kerbs and crawling great trucks'.

THE
VAUXHALL
MOTORIST

Published by
VAUXHALL MOTORS LIMITED
at Edgware Road, The Hyde, LONDON, N.W.9
Telephone : Colindale 6501.   Telegrams : Carvaux Hyde London
Head Office and Works : Luton, Beds

ce Twopence
ol. 1.   No. 1
ober · 1933

AMY171

1 Front cover detail from Issue 1, Volume 1 of *Vauxhall Motorist* magazine in 1933, auspicious in many ways as the Hitler years commenced. This image shows an elegant lady, quintessentially English, in front of a handsome new Light Six Vauxhall. (Vauxhall Motors)

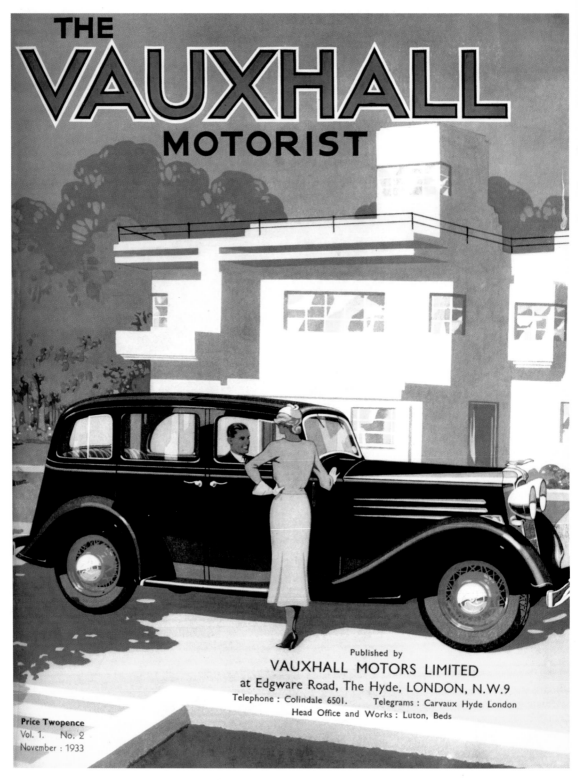

2 This mid-1930s *Vauxhall Motorist* cover panders to the view that women are the vainest of creatures with cars offering further opportunities for their posing. (*Vauxhall Motorist*)

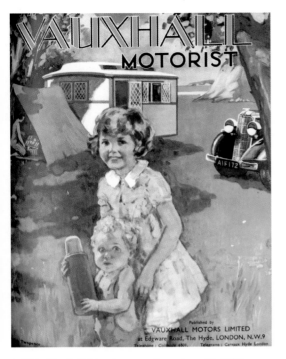

The new **Vauxhall** 20·60

ENCLOSED MOTOR CARS

3 This *Vauxhall Motorist* cover from the mid-1930s depicts the pleasures of camping in a still very rural Britain before another 'great war' that would sweep so much of the old life away. (*Vauxhall Motorist*)

4 This early thirties poster revealed the shape of things to come, notably an end to the popularity of the open topper. But Vauxhall designs still favoured the larger type. (Vauxhall Motors)

5 This Vauxhall Viscount sets off this image of the rural idyll in 1965. The model was popular in New Zealand. (Vauxhall Motors)

6 *Above*: The 1960s evolved into the age of hippies and flower power, largely as a backlash against the Vietnam War by the middle class youth of America who opposed it. The gentle imagery of the era is captured in this interesting woodland shot of a girl with spinning wheel, alongside an HB Viva. (Vauxhall Motors)

7 *Opposite top*: The beautiful young lady is enough to distract us from the pleasant lines of this Victor 101, new for 1963. (Vauxhall Motors)

8 *Opposite bottom*: The HB Viva and HB90 Brabham Viva appeared in 1966, the type including an estate and four door. This model, in period dress, displays the comfort of the de luxe version's roomy front seats and upholstery. (Vauxhall Motors)

11 A new Vectra with a difference: it was the last car to roll off the Luton production line in March 2002. Proud workers surrounded the line for this picture, though anger had been expressed around the town against global capitalists who appeared, to them, careless about making decisions that would affect many lives. GM also laid off 2,000 workers in Germany and Vauxhall chairman Nick Reilly had previously warned the government that there would be job losses if Britain remained outside the Euro. Incidentally, the Vectra 1.8 Sxi has been named 'Used Car of the Year' by *What Car* magazine. The magazines judges were impressed by its value for money. At two years old and with 30,000 miles on the clock, it could be bought for half the original £16,000 price. The Vauxhall Corsa topped the league for super minis.

9 *Opposite top*: The ultra modern Vauxhall HQ in Osborne Road Luton, close to the company's roots in Kimpton Road where Izuzi Bedford Vehicles still keep the GM flag flying locally. (Vauxhall Motors)

10 *Opposite bottom*: A Fronterra of Avon Ambulance NHS Trust. This image shows that it is not just a rugged face, but a very practical vehicle. (Vauxhall Motors)

12 The Lotus built VX220 fitted with Vauxhall's ECOTEC V6. The VX name stays alive, even if the original bonnet flutes had disappeared back in the 1950s, along with the E type. (Robert Cook)

13 The VX Lightning parked alongside some of the company's earlier competition models in the Heritage Centre. (Robert Cook)

CHAPTER SIX

A CAR FOR EVERYONE

Britain was still very much a class divided society by the end of the 1940s, though the new secondary schools did a little to improve the general skills base. Motorists were still mainly middle class or higher, while production line workers could only dream of owning what they helped to build. Nevertheless, aspirations were rising. Cars could be a statement of individuality as well as means of transport. *Vauxhall Motorist* brimmed with lucky fellow's tales of how they individualised and enjoyed their cars. Sometimes they wrote in on the most peculiar matters, such as E.A. Cullen of London, SE9:

> 'The following idea may interest some of your users of the "14" Vauxhall. In the boot of the car at the forward end there are six bars of channel metal, and when luggage of the better leather quality is carried it is liable to chafe against these bars and get damaged. To overcome this drawback I cut strips of rubber matting (quite easily obtained) to the requisite length and width of the bars and secured them by means of metal screws and cup washers (four screws to each bar). A light smear of "Bostik" ensures positive location. This makes a very neat job. It prevents damage to luggage and avoids the rubbing off of any paint, which ultimately leads to rust.'

Vauxhall owners' comments were of undoubted value to model development, a process increasingly complicated in the post-war world. Before 1939 a car could be designed just for the home market. After 1945 it was of vital importance that a car should be acceptable to buyers in many foreign countries with widely varying conditions and against far more severe competition than would be met on the home front. Nevertheless, the car still had to suit the needs of people in Britain. Vauxhall's first response to this challenge was the L type. This was available as the six-cylinder Velox and four-cylinder Wyvern, replacing the 12 and 14hp models.

Released to dealers in August 1948, the model had taken 2½ years to develop and over a million man hours, preparing for sheet metal components and sets of dies. With identical body shells, and recessed headlamps, the Velox and Wyvern went on sale for £430 (plus £120 3s 11d purchase tax) and £350 (plus £97 19s 5d purchase tax) respectively. The L Type's body mascot and wing tips were set closer together to harmonise with new bonnet flutes and the driving compartment was

The 10,000th pre-war H type reaches its 10,000th unit, and had a new lease of life post war until 1948, though many went overseas to help the export drive. (Vauxhall Motors)

built around the driver's needs with a single piece seat with tension springing and carefully positioned spring spoked steering wheel, allowing a clear view of instruments which were all directly in front of the driver's position. The gear lever was set around 2in below the left hand as it rested on the wheel making the most frequent change from top to second very easy, by flicking the lever upwards and back again. Completing the modern interior was a roomy glove compartment, an internal bonnet catch, curved rear window, a large driver's window and push button radio. Reversing lights were optional and advertised as an ideal Christmas present. The Velox was described as being designed for four large people, with an exceptional power to weight ratio, high engine torque at slow speeds, effortless cruising at over one mile a minute, 10-30mph in eight seconds, plus good petrol economy of 25-28mpg at 30mph and driven hard it still managed over 20mpg. Ongoing fuel rationing made fuel economy vital. The Wyvern did even better, being designed to cover 33-35mpg at normal speeds. It handled much like the Velox. The four-cylinder engine was basically the same as the six and could cruise at 55mph with a top speed of 65mph. The Velox offered high torque at low speeds and 106ft pounds at the maximum of 1,600rpm, pulling effortlessly in top gear from maximum speed down to 10mph.

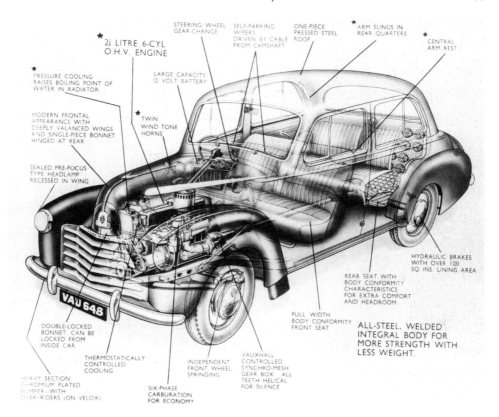

This diagram shows some inner details of the new L type Vauxhall. The model built on the style and advances of the previous H, I and J types. (*Vauxhall Motorist*)

The car also offered considerable climate control for its era. As *Motor* magazine observed:

'You can choose your own climate. The combined heating and windscreen de-icing unit designed specifically for the new Vauxhall Velox and Wyvern offers real driving comfort and increased safety for an outlay of 38. Supplies of the new unit restricted until recently, are now becoming more plentiful and Vauxhall dealers can give reasonably prompt delivery.'

Customers were quick to inform *Vauxhall Motorist* of their views. F.L. Simmons wrote in October 1948:

'So it has happened at last! The latest Vauxhalls in their "new look" dress are out and about. I had feared at first that I should feel obliged to have commenced this letter with such words as "the worst has happened" But I must admit with pleasure that their new lines definitely grow on one.'

However, he went on to criticise the boot and tool box layout, recommending a cover to protect luggage.

The new L type, looking very at home in the countryside having conveyed this attractive couple to a picnic spot. (Vauxhall Motors)

The *Motor* magazine evaluated the Velox in their December 1948 edition, thus:

'In marketing the Velox model for 1949, Vauxhall Motors Limited are setting out to overcome popular prejudice. Their attempt is well timed, and after 600 miles experience of their latest car we feel it fully deserves to succeed. Initial public reactions to the six cylinder model as we have noted them in parking places and elsewhere, are very frequently "what a small car for 18hp". The fact that, with all new cars taxed at annual flat rate of £10 irrespective of size, nominal horse power ratings have lost much of their significance, is as yet by no means universally realised. The fairer reaction to the Vauxhall Velox is, we feel, very different. Acceleration, in top gear or through the gears, matching contemporary American standards, plus generous space for four people and their luggage, with a petrol consumption of 25mpg or better, is quite something. Add six cylinder smoothness and the reliability which should result from the wide use of proven components and the result would be highly attractive at a far higher price than £430 plus purchase tax'.

The report added that the car was a good starter from cold. The driving seat's pivot mountings provided an almost friction-less spring counter balance for the bench seat, which is locked by an accessible lever in the driving side of the car, and the alligator bonnet gave easy access to oil and water filters, the overhead valve gear and down-draught carburettor.

Autocar reported on their Wyvern road test in January, observing that it was almost identical to the Velox, except for the engine, making comparisons inevitable. But,

'the point of the Wyvern is that it offers still greater economy of running costs, a direction in which particularly as regards fuel consumption Vauxhalls show up very favourably, whilst of course the initial price is lower, the Wyvern, indeed being the fourth-lowest priced model on the home market and decidedly roomiest and biggest engined British car at its price.

The report also noted that the 12hp Wyvern offered 'lightness of control and readiness of acceleration derived from a power to weight ratio which is good in the Wyvern...'

At this time the country was hearing about a forthcoming Motorways Bill, to create fuel-saving routes. Running the nation's vehicles was costing £648,000,000 a year, representing 7½ per cent of national income, or £13 per person. With fuel restrictions and so many vehicles going abroad, annual mileage was low by modern standards at 18,000 million, working out at 9*d* a mile. However, with many new towns to be built, high growth was expected and better roads would reduce accidents – Oxfordshire's three-year study had suggested that 59 per cent of accidents were due to road defects.

There was also news of a project to build a 3,300ft Severn Bridge halfway between Bristol and Gloucester and AA introduced a radio controlled breakdown service. *Vauxhall Motorist* reported in January/February 1953:

'Motorists in the London area who need to call on the Automobile Association for assistance may in future be astonished at the speed with which help arrives. At the first stage in the introduction of a national radio network that will provide continuous two-way verbal communication between AA patrols and their local headquarters, the Association has inaugurated a radio patrol service covering an area of approximately twenty miles around Fanum House. Patrols will be directed by radio to any motorist telephoning for assistance... The radio patrols are a logical extension of the Association's radio-controlled night breakdown services which have been operating in London, Birmingham and Leeds for sometime...'

The *Vauxhall Motorist* reported in January/February 1953 upon the case for better roads:

'The welter of road statistics with which the British public are bombarded reveal a dismal picture. Exactly how dismal that picture is depends on whether the figures are presented by Government officials (who talk in terms of increased expenditure on roads over last year) or by road user organisations who are inclined to compare the proportion of motor tax income spent on roads this year with the proportion spent on roads at some previous stage of motoring history.'

While the government dithered, car development raced ahead. Frank Ford recalled:

'I got a thorough grounding in vehicle engineering at Vauxhall. I went from the running shop into the testing section. There were a number of cars that needed maintenance. Two engine test rigs were in the tank shop, where the Vauxhall retail park is now. I had eight months gathering work experience and on to the engineering drawing office for six-seven years and back to the experimental department where I became an experimental engineer. The hierarchy had the Chief Engineer and his assistant at the top. Below them were the passenger and commercial vehicle engineers and they had their experimental engineers who did the actual work. In the passenger vehicle section, we had control of a fleet of other makes of cars that were in competition with ours. We were out to assess, not copy them, looking at matters such as roominess.'

Post-war Vauxhalls were being well received worldwide. Les Coleman recalls their popularity in his native Australia:

'While serving in the RAAF at Laverton, Victoria, I purchased a 1948 model Vauxhall Wyvern tourer. I think it only had one owner before me and was in excellent condition. It was blue, looked great and was my pride and joy. In those days not many young guys had cars and mine was one of only five cars owned by airman (only officers normally had cars) at Laverton RAAF station. In the summer, with it being a tourer, it really got the birds. I never had so many friends after buying this car. I was posted to RAAF station Ballarat and was in great demand with people looking for a lift to Melbourne at weekends (mostly WAAFs). The Vauxhall was a very simple car to work on yourself and I could take off the head, do a de coke and valve grind easily in a day. Most maintenance you could do yourself, not like today's cars. A friend of mine bought a new Vauxhall Velox tourer which was similar to the Wyvern, but had a 6-cylinder engine. One time I was returning to Ballarat at night and a car coming toward me would not dip his lights so I flashed mine and as he passed I was in total darkness. My headlights had failed. Being on a bend at the time, I ran off the road on the wrong side, somehow went between two posts and stopped about one foot from a drop into a gully. Quite frightening! On checking found that the fuse had blown. We finished up following behind a bus to get back to Ballarat. One problem with the Wyvern was the brakes. The road from Ballarat to Melbourne in those days was just a single lane each way and went through the Pentland Hills. Coming down the brakes would fade and it became a very exciting descent as the speed increased and the brakes became almost useless. On another occasion the passenger side door came open, and as they opened backwards, it tore the door off. The bodywork on these cars was a wooden frame and it was badly broken. Fortunately my uncle worked at Floods Body builders in St Kilda Road and was able to repair it for me.'

Les Coleman and fellow Australians were enjoying rather more prosperity than those back in the mother country. As Britain entered the 1950s, style and comfort was the dream of many, inspired by television and film images from the USA. Americans had no need for austerity and were eager to enjoy life. General Motors was doing well at home and abroad, with inevitable benefit to Vauxhall's progress. Building on the impressive L Type's achievements, Vauxhall delivered the E Type in 1951, a full body shell available in several variants, including basic Velox and

Wyvern and still sporting bonnet flutes that went back to the company's earliest designs. Some, like Mr G.E. Fisher of Bolton, Lancs, personalised their cars, using a range of accessories on sale. In his case a local body builder was called in to modify the boot lid, creating a huge bulge so that he could carry a demonstration bacon slicer around his sales pitch!

Bench seating accommodated six passengers. Easy clean but expensive leather upholstery gave way to synthetic, prompting one reader to contact *Vauxhall Motorist* with the question: 'How can I remove ink stains from the back seat of my Velox, the upholstery is vyanide?' The answer was clean water if recent, virtually impossible if not.

A column shift gear change operated the three-speed transmission and steering was by worm and peg while suspension was independent by wishbones and coils at the front, and on the rear semi elliptical. The Velox version was a low priced 2,262cc six-cylinder car, with an optional high compression engine available. Offering effortless performance and fuel economy of 25mpg, it cost £535 plus purchase tax of £224 0s 10d. Weighing 22.5cwt it had a maximum speed of 82mph on the flat and 69mph on a 1 in 20 gradient. Acceleration through the gears, at 13.6 secs, to 50mph was good for the early 1950s. The car would run at 17.9mph in top, at 1,000 rpm. *Autocar* commented:

'There may be some who will trace a strong American suggestion about the new Velox and liken it to a 2¼ litre version of the transatlantic conception of American motoring...'

Undoubtedly the car looked like a scaled-down GM model from the US and was consequently attractive to the style conscious in still drab Britain.

Britain was still struggling to find a place in a world it once dominated, but a Conservative Government was more minded to boost home consumption, although they did not forsake Labour's basic planning strategy. The Festival of Britain in 1951 was a brave attempt to boost confidence, but the 300ft Skylon feature was likened to the economy as having no visible means of support. Rationing and other restrictions were gradually abandoned. In this easier environment Vauxhall produced 110,099 vehicles in 1953, over 40,000 being delivered to the home market, while 66,300 (62.2 per cent) went abroad, many to the Commonwealth. The home delivery export service, run from Wardour Street, London, was an initiative to help the individual buyers like Bill Smith, a Ceylon tea planter. Bill had ordered his car in Colombo, collecting it while on six months leave. Wardour took care of shipping details, arranging delivery within the necessary six months to avoid purchase tax. Vauxhalls were the car to have in the old colonies as Les Coleman poignantly recalls from Australia:

'In 1953 the RAAF posted me to Korea and I left my precious Vauxhall in the care of a friend who was going to look after it. Unbeknown to me, my mother decided to learn to drive in my car. On return to Australia, I of course found this out and also found the car was not running very well. In fact it was almost useless. It blew smoke and kept oiling up the plugs.

Sir Charles Bartlett, chairman and MD, enjoys his part in the company's fifty years of car making celebrations. (Vauxhall Motors)

Somehow it looked a different colour than I remembered but was assured it was just as I had left it. On pulling into a service station for petrol the owner said he would never forget the car as it had been badly dented. As they could not match the paint, they had to repaint the whole car! Of course mother had to own up to her bad driving, but I never found out how she could have wrecked the engine. At that stage it was time to move on to something else, but the Wyvern was the best car, enjoyment wise, that I ever owned.'

British roads still left much to be desired and a paltry increase of £10 million spending per annum made little difference. J. Anthony Edwards used the *Vauxhall Motorist* to inform readership that:

'The history of British roads over the last half century is a history of cheese paring and muddle that has left the country with a highway system years behind the vehicles that use it...'

The magazine was still complaining in April 1955:

'Our road system is completely inadequate, wasteful of time and money and a serious hazard to safety. Industry must have quick and efficient transportation. Our road system must be modernised so that these needs can be met.

Vauxhall L type getting the 'once over' in a local dealer's garage. (Vauxhall Motors)

Meanwhile, Lancashire police, famous for the Z cars TV take off, was turning away from beat policemen, running over 400 vehicles and covering 6.25 million miles per year. From 1951-53 the force added thirty-three Veloxes and seven Wyverns to its fleet, police drivers praising the Velox for its road holding at speeds up to 80mph. With more high performing cars on the road and a steady rise in vehicle crime, Vauxhall was making a big contribution to catching the law breakers. Ever more vehicle legislation also added to the traffic cops' burden. In April 1953, the Transport Lighting Act became law, requiring that vehicles have two rear lights and reflectors 1.5in in diameter. Along with goods vehicles under 30cwt, car rear lights had to be not less than 21in apart.

A range of accessories were advertised in March 1953 to 'Give your Vauxhall the Coronation look. Sparkling new chromium to make your Vauxhall worthy of the great occasion.' New bonnet flutes cost from £1, new badges 10s 6d, bonnet mascots 18s 6d, new over riders 25s a pair, bumper bars from 77s 6d, hub caps from 18s 6d. There was even the Eccles Lightweight Coronation caravan. London bus driver S.G. Bull was commissioned to advise *Vauxhall Motorist* readers intending to visit the capital for Coronation celebrations not to overtake buses on the inside because they do not have trafficators. He advised visitors to leave their cars in suburban garages.

As the new monarch was crowned, Vauxhall's own long-reigning monarch resigned. *Vauxhall Motorist* reported:

'The news that Sir Charles Bartlett is relinquishing the Managing Director's chair of Vauxhall Motors was sad news for the people who work for Vauxhall – and unexpected news. It was known that Sir Charles reaches the Company's retirement age next year but no one had expected an announcement of the kind that has just been released... He believed in gradually relinquishing executive responsibility. He had been a guiding hand for twenty-five years, staying as chair and handing over to Mr Walter Hill, an American citizen born in England of English parents and previously with key General Motors appointments in America, New Zealand and Australia. A Vauxhall Director since 1949, he takes over on June 1st. Charles Bartlett was Managing Director from 1930, expanding the plant from eleven acres with 2,000 employees and 1,400 vehicles built per year, to eighty-fiev acres, 12,000 employees and 100,000 vehicles per year.'

The world moved on and *Vauxhall Motorist* reported:

'1953 will go down in the history of Vauxhall Motors as a year of celebration and achievement. It was the fiftieth anniversary of the production of the first Vauxhall car; it saw for the first time, the annual production rate stepped up to more than 100,000 vehicles.'

A green Velox (an E Type) was the 100,000th vehicle driven off the production line that year. Arthur had driven the company's 100,000th vehicle ever off the production line nineteen years earlier.

It seems astonishing how much the company had evolved in such a short time, and now a world away from the time when John Smith's father paid £100 to indenture his son to Vauxhall in 1903 while the boy 'earned' 2s 6d. (27½p) to learn the 'art of the trade'. There was no specialisation then, cars were built by teams and conditions were harder. By 1953, there were 350 apprentices on the payroll, compared to six in 1903. These people would often go on to become supervisors in quality control and some were trained to service the cars – a role originally fulfilled by blacksmiths. The *Vauxhall Motorist* editorial proudly commented in September 1953;

'when you have completed fifty years at anything – be it staying married, staying unmarried, or what you like – you are entitled to sit back for a moment and preen yourself a little. And so we make no apology for the fact that this issue tends to harp somewhat on one theme. It is fifty years ago that the first Vauxhall took the road... We envy the men who, when another fifty years have passed, will have the job of reviewing the first century in the history of the Vauxhall car; they will have a truly great story to tell.'

The year 1953 was thus momentous for Vauxhall, their magazine reporting:

'If you lose touch with a friend at this year's Earls Court Motor Show, you stood a pretty poor chance of finding him again. Even seasoned show veterans like manufacturers

Bedford was not going to be left behind in the glamour stakes as this image from the Earls Court Commercial Motor Show makes clear, featuring a new light coach being used by Miss Great Britain. If only more Beefeaters looked like her there would be a rush of people wanting to be locked up in the Tower of London with them! (Vauxhall Motors)

representatives admitted to being somewhat impressed with the size of the crowds this year. The total attendance was of course a record – 612, 953... the Vauxhall stand was again one of the main centres of attraction. If an artist had been around who wanted to paint a human representation of "wishful thinking", he would have found a plentiful supply of subjects around the turntable on which a Caribbean blue Velox rotated in stately glory, all he wouldn't have found was empty space to set up his easel.' The show was opened by the Duke of Edinburgh.'

New Vauxhalls featured a new recalculating ball type steering gear, with a single start worm gear welded to the inner steering column. The rugged, but stylish design made them popular all rounders. Around Cardiff and Swansea, the E Type Wyverns were a common sight in the fleets of Glamtax, the largest operator in South Wales, and also Streamline of Swansea. The latter's twelve Wyverns all had roof racks, heaters and reversing lights. Other bulk users included the Car Hire Group at London Airport and the Co-op undertakers in Newcastle and Portsmouth.

The E type Vauxhall, style showing the Detroit influence but retaining the famous bonnet flutes and pictured in picturesque Bath. The E type was the last model to feature a fluted bonnet. (Vauxhall Motors)

Letters praising the E type were plentiful. George C. Jackson wrote from Beirut:

'I have a Vauxhall Velox 1951. I am really very satisfied with it. I like very much its powerful top gear, its powerful brakes and in general terms its solidity and comfort. Otherwise it takes an honourable place in our country among a great number of cars from other nations like France, Italy, Germany and among the other British cars too.'

No detail was too small for consideration in the pages of the *Vauxhall Motorist*, as Miss R. Beer's letter from 1953 attests:

'Dear Sir, I overcame the difficulty of fixing the AA badges etc. on my Wyvern by buying a chromium towel rail and slightly bending it in the centre, fixing it to the car with fittings supplied, standing these on end to take the rail there is still plenty of room for more badges.'

From Jamaica, F.A.C. Taylor wrote:

'I am enclosing a picture of my 1950 Vauxhall Wyvern. The performance of this car is such that I would not be doing justice to it if I kept silent. As an Inspector of Police (I am now

The E type Vauxhall showing its colours in an African rally. (Vauxhall Motors)

retired) I travelled 500 miles per month over some of the roughest roads in the Island and have always reached my destination. Gas consumption is 38mpg, which I consider excellent and up to the present the car has travelled 28,000 miles without trouble. I hope you continue turning out machines that will give the satisfaction the 1950 Vauxhalls are giving, as some of my friends get 40mpg. Here's to the success of the later Vauxhall models.'

Another reader wrote anxiously:

'I would value some advice concerning my 1955 Velox. I am experiencing a "sizzling" noise which when sitting in my driver's seat appears to be under the facia...'

The bemused reply suggested that: 'It appears to be the radio grille. Tape it up.' Other letters of that year included news of a 27hp E Type that could still knock up 70mph, with 231,693 miles on the clock and another about the greatly improved appearance of a Velox when fitted with bumper over riders.

Vauxhalls were popular towing cars and a caravanner's frequent choice. The company would also dominate the market for small camper vans based on the CA van conversion by Martin Walter Ltd of Folkestone. The CA was designed by David Jones, the company's longest-serving design executive. This radical van

Golden Jubilee

What superlatives, we wonder, would the motorist of 1903 have lavished on these latest Vauxhalls, with their breathtaking acceleration into the seventies, and beyond, their exceptional road-holding at speed and their effortless cruising. Here, indeed, are comfort and performance undreamed of when the first Vauxhall made its debut 50 years ago . . . motoring that even today is ahead of its time.

In 1903, the Vauxhall owner was a hardy pioneer. He had to be. Today, he enjoys a degree of luxury, reliability, and pride of ownership his forbears would scarcely have believed possible.

In 1903 his "accessories" were polar dress and an umbrella. Today he can have radio, built in heating and ventilation, a windscreen washer and other aids, all "tailored" exclusively for his car and his comfort.

Yes, the motorist of half a century back would surely hail these newest Vauxhalls as a triumph of Vauxhall achievement, the culmination of fifty years of engineering leadership. Today, as in 1903, Vauxhall leads the way.

VAUXHALL MOTORS LTD.
LUTON · BEDS

Printed in Great Britain by HUNT, BARNARD & CO., LTD., Aylesbury, and Published by the Proprietors
VAUXHALL MOTORS LTD., Luton, Bedfordshire.   September/October, 1953.

Golden Jubilee edition cover of *Vauxhall Motorist*. (Vauxhall Motors)

The Bedford CA van was a stalwart of the newspaper industry. This one wears the livery of the *Evening News*. (Vauxhall Motors)

survived with various modifications well into 1969, being particularly popular in the news distribution industry, and with small traders and builders. If someone wanted a little more style than a van, Martin Walter was already producing a Velox Dormobile conversion in 1956, for £741 plus £371 17s purchase tax and the Grovesnor estate for £750 plus £376 7s tax. By contrast the CA Bedford Utilabrake was a mere £573 10s 0d, but it attracted no purchase tax.

More and more of Britain was being opened up to motoring. The first US-style Motel opened at Kenilworth. It was called 'Round Towers Auto Villas' because it was built in the grounds of a Victorian mansion known as 'Round Towers' and offering luxury at low cost. Foreign holidays were becoming popular again, but as John Hartley observed in his article 'All for one pound per person' in *Vauxhall Motorist*, May/June 1954:

'Let us be quite honest about this: There is a lot of booking and form filling, preparation and general "coping" to be done before a caravan holiday in Europe can be enjoyed. But my wife and I, both complete novices at the game, tackled the job successfully. We took our 1953 Velox, our two schoolgirl daughters, Rosemary and June, and Eccles 'Alert' caravan for a twenty-six-day holiday on the continent, covered some 2,652 miles, spent less than we expected, and thoroughly enjoyed ourselves...'

The Bedford CA Dormobile was a home from home and much less of a burden to drive and locate than a cumbersome car and caravan. Such luxury was expensive: £1,112 17 shillings. (Vauxhall Motors)

Vauxhall annual production topped 100,000 by the end of 1954, total income was £66,827,365, total expenses £59,965,737, with a net profit of £6,861,628 and taxes paid of £15 million. The November/December 1954 editorial of *Vauxhall Motorist* informed readers:

'What's new to the public is history to the designers. The three new models are the outcome of many months of patient designing, re-designing, testing and research, carried out by Vauxhall's experts to make absolutely sure that the cars will be as good as they look. Part of this testing took place in sunny Spain, where the dust is blinding and dense.'

Testing at home could be more awkward, as Frank Ford recalled:

'Before we had our own proving ground we did high speed testing on public roads. The A41 Aylesbury to Bicester was a popular choice. I was doing this one day, with the fifth wheel attached – the fifth wheel was a very accurate speedometer, to within one-three per cent. Then suddenly a police car came along. The policeman said: "I don't know what the rules are with one wheel trailers. It's 40mph with two." "Your boss and mine can write to each other and perhaps you can do it elsewhere". I said, "where do you suggest?"'

Traffic rules were tightening throughout the 1950s. The 1955 Traffic Bill introduced compulsory vehicle inspections, rules for the parking and removal of vehicles by the police if causing obstruction, and the first tests of mechanical fitness of vehicles, establishing the first test stations. The age of the parking meter

For those who wanted car comfort combined with Dormobile style convenience, this E type with fold down double-bed conversion by Martin Walter was just the thing. By this time Walter, who adopted the Dormobile trade name, had nearly 350 years experience in coach building. They started out building phaetons and barouches. They never did anything but luxury coach work.

had arrived. Up until this time pedestrians could only be prosecuted for loitering at a zebra crossing and obstructing the free flow of traffic. From here on they could be in trouble if they infringed rules enshrined in the new Highway Code – which was issued to every motorist. The code contained vital knowledge on legal proceedings and for deciding liability.

The age of mass motoring made reforms urgent. Prime Minister Churchill made way for Anthony Eden, whose first show as Conservative leader gained 49.7 per cent of the votes, making a solid base to carry on modernising Britain. There were a lot of fairly affordable cars on the market, offering lots of competition for Vauxhall, the Morris Minor 1000 being a particular favourite of the increasingly affluent working class who could use them for weekend jaunts out to a country pub. Steak houses like the first Berni Inn at Bristol set the pace for post war road life, a far cry from 1930s picnics. The car was also something of a passion wagon, the E Type Vauxhall being the chosen love nest for Michael Caine in the film 'Alfie' a few years later. Britain was getting a little more glamorous at last and Vauxhall announced profits of £6,542,467 from an income of £75,640,795 in 1955. Taxes paid by the company to help the struggling nation, and its dubious foreign policy, were £4,282,444.

There can be no doubt that this mature couple are enjoying life on a British camp site. If we are old enough, we can easily imagine all the pleasures in store for them when they go visiting the local beauty spots, shops and tea shops. (Vauxhall Motors)

In keeping with the new world, and very much a sign of the times, manufacturers started offering a deluxe model or special equipment versions of their production models. Such was the E Type Vauxhall Cresta, being basically a special equipment version of the Velox, the radiator grille restyled too. The Cresta had many additional fittings and a range of distinctive two-tone finishes. It was still basically a family car, but included a high compression cylinder head giving a ratio of 7:3 instead of the standard 6:5. The engine was six-cylinder, 2,262 cc, push rod. Weight was 23 cwt, fuel tank 56 gallons, turning circle 38ft, with coil spring and wishbone front independent suspension. The increased performance lifted the model from the bread and butter family saloon class, creating more appeal to those who enjoy driving for its own sake and who, for family and business reasons, had to forego a sports car. For all this extra, the car was a competitively priced £595 plus £249 0s 10d. Extras included a radio for £21 plus £4 7s 11d tax. For those who could not afford a new car there was a 'new engines for old' scheme for all types back to the pre-war '10', offered at competitive prices, with genuine parts and six months' guarantee.

With so much to offer, there had to be more expansion, so began a £36 million scheme, announced in 1954, including doubling the education and training centre at a cost of £130,000, increasing the intake of apprentices from fifty-four per

Bedford truck assembly line at Dunstable a few miles from Luton, in its first year during which 50,000 Bedfords were built. (Vauxhall Motors)

Pleasant seating and gardens set the tone for the new Dunstable truck assembly plant. (Vauxhall Motors)

Aerial view of the Dunstable truck and van plant, a strikingly linear facility compared to the more cramped confines of the original Luton factory. (Vauxhall Motors)

year to 125. The new centre would have 32,000sq.ft of floor space compared with 14,900. At any time, the centre would have 350 apprentices, with a staff of thirty instructors. Sadly, retired MD Sir Charles Bartlett, born back in 1889 when Vauxhall were still making steam engines, did not live to see this. He died at his Harpenden home, the *Vauxhall Motorist* noting in memorium:

'His natural ability was developed by his life long study of the human problems in industry and it is for his interest in people that he will be chiefly remembered. Many of the practices now accepted in industry, Sir Charles pioneered... His thoughts and energies were concentrated on the well being of this company for almost thirty years.'

The new expansion phase was building on foundations created during the Bartlett years. The plan was to raise production from 130,000 to 250,000 vehicles, requiring massive excavation into the Chiltern hillside, opening an area equal to thirteen football pitches as well as work underway for the new and separate truck plant in Dunstable. Spoil from the Luton site was used to extend the airport and reclaim thirty-two acres of Luton Hoo Park. Steel work came from the United States, having been intended for a wartime GMC plant that was making B-29 bombers. Overall, there would be an additional 3 million square feet of floor space added to the 3.5 million square feet in Luton and 1,630,000 to the 264,000sq.ft already established at the Dunstable truck assembly plant. Dunstable also gained a 130ft water tower, based on a US idea and the largest in Britain. This was going to free up space for car production at Luton. A colossal L-shaped block, covering 1,432,000sq.ft, two thirds the size of the wartime factory, rose up across the old sports field. This was a state of the art facility, equal to anything in the United States, with a huge basement and the largest press shop in Europe. The new AA block was among the largest steel frame structures of the day. Vauxhall were preparing themselves for the true age of popular motoring and a car for everyone.

CHAPTER SEVEN

NEVER HAD IT SO GOOD

The 1956 Wyvern was basically the same as its predecessor, except it had the added appeal of two-tone vynide and calfskin upholstery – a vinyl-coated woven fabric, improved trim, cast-iron brake drums to increase braking efficiency, having increased the front ratio from 59:41 to 64:36. The Wyvern and Velox was also available in nine new exterior colour combinations and with a new instrument panel. The new model also had no need of the old 'running in please pass' stickers so commonplace in the back windows of new cars.

The mass production process was becoming much faster while car design and modification lagged. Maurice Platt, director and Chief Engineer of Vauxhall Motors wrote in the *Motor* on 18 May 1955:

'In the carefree days of the 1920s it was not considered particularly outrageous to decide upon a new model in July, rush a prototype into production early in the year following. Nowadays, it is a fairly safe bet that by the time that the large scale manufacture of a new car commences, the specification and styling are already at least two years old.'

Many, however, like Viking Taxis in Denmark, were very happy with the old specifications, informing the company:

'One of our cars has covered 162,800 miles with no engine work. Surely this is a record and an engineering triumph for your firm?'

Platt went on to explain that an approved design had to hold its own in a competitive world and there is a lot of design and expense in setting up the dies and tools for efficient volume production. Upon forecasting the future, he wrote:

'In general, the process just described consists of close scrutiny of the existing situation and a careful assessment of the factors which are likely to alter the situation over a period optimistically referred to as the foreseeable future...'

Petrol supplies were once again threatened when President Nasser seized the Suez Canal, regardless of the Anglo French efforts to dissuade the Egyptians.

Vauxhall heyday in the early 1950s, the workers turn out of the busy factory wedged in a hollow on the Chiltern hillside. (Vauxhall Motors)

Early optimism was reflected in headlines like 'It's Great Britain Again', but it was not to be so. In spite of ration certificates being printed again, the march of the motorist was not unduly upset. *Motor* road-tested the Vauxhall Cresta, reporting in October 1956:

> 'Turning ...now to a consideration of the Cresta in absolute terms as distinct from making comparisons with predecessors one calls to mind the statement: "Happy is the country with no history" for this is an unremarkable car for the good reason that it embraces a large number of practical fittings and none that are there by reason of tradition or sentiment, it had a good road performance completely in harmony with that of modern traffic; and neutral qualities of handling which make it a safe and comfortable car making little demand on the driver's intelligence or attention...

The year 1957 was something of a turning point for style and development. New models had to be disguised for testing on the open road and in 1956 Frank Ford had been up to his old tricks racing one of the new FA Type Vauxhall Victors at maximum speed between Acle and Great Yarmouth. Luckily for him the traffic cops were as scarce as they are today and there were no speed cameras. 'We never got warned off using this road and we still hadn't got out test track built.'

The Vauxhall Victor, posed with its namesake RAF Victor nuclear bomber, reminding us that Britain was still pursuing an expensive foreign policy in 1957. (Vauxhall Motors)

The year 1957 had special significance for marking the centenary of the Vauxhall name. A brand new 1.5 million acres of factory was ready for action and new designs would mark the occasion as the Wyvern made way for the F Type Victor and the two new PA Sixes (Velox and Cresta) were made ready for production in the new advanced plant. Exciting new body shapes required complex new presses and there were 225 of these, all but three being British-built. Much of the old manhandling in production had been replaced by mechanical. Most of the steel was delivered in coil form, with 1,000 tons pressed weekly. The FA and PA production involved a complex system of co-ordinated conveyors covering a distance of 1.75 miles. The line was designed for quality and volume, delivering thirty-one body shells hourly. Bodies were built on a series of forty-two special jig trucks, moving slowly on the 828ft floor conveyor, capable of carrying the three current model bodies: Victor, Victor estate and Cresta/Velox. Sections of underbody were assembled on nearby press welding machines. The complete floor and side frames were built up on the jigs, twenty-eight pairs moving alongside the conveyors, other overhead conveyors delivered body panels in synchronisation. Timing was meticulous

The new sixes were long and low, a good 4½in lower than predecessors and with stunning panoramic windscreens with 6.5sq.ft of glass with pillars out of the line of view. All three new models had been developed through hard testing at home and abroad.

Once again it is Motor Show time and the new FA Victors and PA Crestas look good alongside some very expensive competition. There was no doubting that Vauxhall offered value for money and aimed its products at the county set. (Vauxhall Motors)

The FA Victor was a new concept in mass motoring. It was a car with the looks of tomorrow, bound to make owners the envy of their neighbours and yet available at a bargain price of £485 for the basic model. According to *Vauxhall Motorist* in March/April 1957, it was:

'a car that is eager under your hands, yet asks little of your pocket. This is the smaller Vauxhall that people all over the world have been waiting for, the answer to the conjecture of years. This is the car by which all others of its class will in future be judged... When the curtain fell at the Gaumont Theatre, Kilburn, London, on the morning of February 7th, a huge audience that included Vauxhall dealers from all over the world knew that they had seen a piece of motoring history in the making. They had watched the introduction to the world of the new Vauxhall Victor. ...they had seen it make its bow as star of the first theatrical production of a new car ever staged in Europe. For two and a half hours they applauded as a cast of over 100 (ranging from Arthur Askey to the Band of the Grendadier Guards) introduced the Victor in a specially written musical show produced by Ralph Reader of Gang Show fame...'

The 166.5in long and 62.16in wide car was a 1.5 litre, four-cylinder with synchromesh on all forward gears, available in various eye-catching colour

Retired Vauxhall development engineer at home in Luton with one of the old Griffin hood ornaments on his lap. He said, 'It always used to face forward until it had to be redesigned to fit in the same circle as Opel's Blitz symbol.' He recalled that the FA and PA series were good cars but had a reputation for rusting and being knee bashers when you got into the front seats. (Vauxhall Motors)

schemes and with ground-breaking panoramic windscreen. Standing 58in high, the FA Victor had a 6in ground clearance. Though compact, there was plenty of room for four inside. The *Manchester Guardian* correspondent wrote:

'I was impressed by the car's road-holding qualities and smoothness of the gearbox.' Fuel consumption would make the car even more attractive, managing 45.4mpg at 20mph, 40.6mpg at 40mph and 35mpg at 50mph.

Vauxhall had always led in the fight for fuel efficiency, able to boast as far back as 1937 that they could offer a car capable of 40mpg. Tommy Wisdom of the *Daily Herald* reckoned:

'It's the best all-round family car yet made by General Motors British factory.'

Vauxhall Motorist advised that:

'Caravan owners will be glad of the special attachment. It is easily fitted and correctly spreads the stresses caused by towing – a must for caravaners and a mere £3.'

The PA on test in the Alps, when the cars were, according to Frank Ford who drove on, 'smothered in sensors.' (Vauxhall Motors)

The car was also a bargain at £485 for the basic model, £505 for the more opulent Super Victor.

Gears were three forward and reverse with the drive line a single open propeller shaft with a needle roller universal joint. Production involved two chemical anti-rust treatments. The under body was effectively sealed by 1/16in plastic skin. Vauxhall also offered an engine operated screen clean for £2 12s 6d.

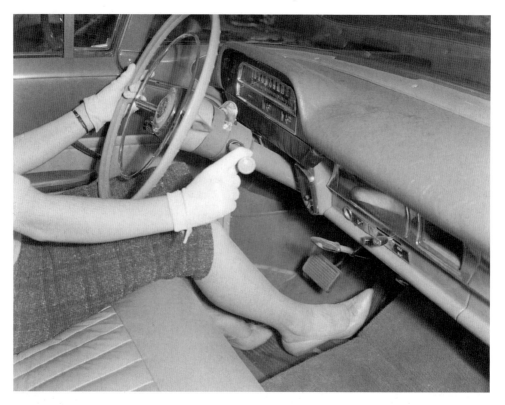

The PA Velox/Cresta 's driving position is clearly displayed in this export version, including the US style bench front seat. (Vauxhall Motors)

Frank Ford, looking back, said: The FA Victor was a great car if only it hadn't rusted. That was GM's fault. Maurice Platt asked Chevrolet to lend us draughtsmen because we were designing the FA and PA – the PA was the basis of the new Cresta and Velox – at the same time. This was a big demand. He wanted twelve draughtsmen and we would pay the hotel bills. They said "no", telling us to send one of our body engineers to them where he would be allocated part of the drawing office. So we ended up with two cars partly designed in the US and here in Luton. Parts of the design begged to rust. The sickle shaped indent in the back door, pockets under the wings and dash all rotted. It took us ten years to get our reputation back for body work after that.' One must take Frank's point, but Vauxhall had been at pains to ensure quality of production in their new plant. Rust proofing and painting was taken most seriously. The process was still heavily dependent on manual skills. Cars involved much detail, having lots of small sheet metal parts, with headlamp cowls and other mouldings to be added to the body at different trim stages. Painting it all was a challenge to the time and cost-saving principle of standardisation with over 600 cars a day, six different models, ten different single colours and thirteen different dual tones. Painting involved five separate processes, each divided into various operations: rust-proofing (phosphating), underbody dipping, primer painting, wet sanding, colour

This image of an unusual left-hand drive version of the FA Victor suggests that it might be en route to an American or Canadian keen to get in touch with his Scots ancestry. Vauxhall had clearly moved away from the concept that you can have any colour so long as it is black! (Vauxhall Motors)

application. Rust-proofing involved twelve operations and the whole business required 3-4 gallons of paint per car, totalling 2,500 gallons per day.

The trim shop – where bodies were finished inside and out, roof and body lineage, seating, floor covering, electrical equipment, steering assemblies and glass – was equally busy and complex by the late 1950s, furnishing 700 cars daily, using nearly three miles of Vynide in sixty-two different colours, patterns and qualities for headlining and seat covering. Carpeting was available in ten different colours, with Vauxhall using over half a mile daily. Wadding was used at the rate of thirteen miles daily, and cowhide from 250 animals was needed for the luxury seating, using fourteen different colourings. The whole business included women operating 200 sewing machines, trim work being mainly hand work. Next the bodies were lowered on to the final assembly.

Soon the car transporters were heading away down the Markyate by-pass loaded with export models. By mid-September 1957 more Vauxhalls had been sold than for the whole of 1956, mainly due to the Victor. In 1955 25 per cent

The Victor was a sort of baby Velox but it was first of the production line, seen here in February 1957. (Vauxhall Motors)

of production went to Europe, in 1957 the figure had reached 38 per cent. Import quotas had restricted exports to Australia but 5,500 went to South Africa compared to 4,650 in 1956. By October 1957, the superb new PA sixes, Cresta and Velox added to Vauxhall's competitive edge. As well as the panoramic windscreen, the PA featured a full-width three-piece rear window to ease the strain of parking such a large car, direction indicators on swept straight through rear wings, tail and stop lights protected by massive bumpers, low broad grille, low centre of gravity and consequent good road holding. The overall effect was very pleasing to the eye. *Automotive News* in Detroit commented in December 1958:

> 'The Vauxhall (Victor) is a car which will speedily remove any erroneous preconceived notions about lack of smoothness in a four cylinder motor… here is a thoroughbred auto. Only the softest touch on the gas pedal zooms it up to 50 then 60. I do not know at what speed the engine would work too hard but I did discover that the Vauxhall was in its natural element at 60-65mph and that you need not lag behind in the parade.'

Miss M. Lofthouse, a secretary in Geneva, won a Victor in a national lottery launched by General Motors Suise SA as part of a Victor sales drive in early

The PA was not far behind the Victor, only a few months. This picture shows the first one of the 1958 batch, reprised at the 1957 Motor Show.

1958. This followed on a record year in 1957 when truck and car exports rose by 33 per cent to 84,500 vehicles – 56,000 cars and 28,500 commercials. From Vauxhall's standpoint, with the best new plant in Europe, 1958 was a year to be approached with zest and enthusiasm. At the same time there was some improvement in road building with the £6 million Ross Spur motorway sweeping from the Midlands into Wales and the Channel Ports motorway from Faversham to Rochester. On 19 May 1958 the 100,000th Victor rolled off the production line. No British car had ever sold in such quantity in the first fifteen months of its production and it is doubtful if any British car had entered so many new overseas territories in such a short time. Exports to the US had begun in September 1957 and the intake was already running at 20,000 a year and record numbers were going to Canada's testing environment.

At the same time the new six-cylinder cars, which under test had achieved 1,071 miles on forty-eight gallons (22.3 mpg), were prospering. The *Motor* reported in June 1958:

Both FA and PA series cars were built in these almost clinical surroundings of Vauxhall's new ultra modern production line. (Vauxhall Motors)

'...this latest Vauxhall Cresta 5/6 seater shows every promise of being a highly successful new model. Smartly fashionable in appearance, but not exaggeratedly flashy, big yet not so bulky as to be a nuisance around towns...'

Autocar reported:

'The latest Vauxhall Cresta and Velox – caters for a wide international market. In spite of its low appearance, it will fit most garages...'

G.A. Swinterton of Solihull, however, did not find his PA Velox completely satisfying. In April 1958 he had it packed with radio equipment to talk throughout the world. Sadly, only limited power could be obtained through the aerial because the car was too low to the ground. Nonetheless, his call sign, G6AS/M penetrated beyond the iron curtain to the jungles of Malaya.

Cecil Siddle of Brynmawr, Brecon, was more than satisfied with his new Vauxhall, as he wrote in August 1958:

'For publication in 'The *Vauxhall Motorist*' I am enclosing a snap of a young lady friend on the bonnet of my Velox. I have been teaching her to drive, and though it's a big car for a

It seems sexist today but the common typical marketing view of the 1950s and 60s was that a glamorous lady would enhance the attractiveness of any new car, thus helping sales. It would still be fairly normal for the average man to find this image an attractive juxtaposition of bodies! (Vauxhall Motors)

learner (a woman at that!) she finds it very easy to handle, after two lessons only. Speaking for myself, I find this model a great improvement on the previous ones. This is my fourth new Vauxhall in five years and they all run trouble free. I usually do at least 30,000 miles a year. Hoping that you will print this snap, if only to lend a little glamour to your magazine.'

Other enthusiasts for the new PA included favourite comedian of the day Fred Emney who named his dog Cresta because, like his car, 'It knows how to behave on the road.'

Success was the result of sound, forward planning and investment. A new two storey engine development building covered 8,000sq.ft, with four dynamometer rooms (measuring engine characteristics), carburation and fuel injection test rooms and offices was added to facilities. The company's commercial side was also breaking new ground advancing truck design, improving the R and S Type Big Bedfords, working on a radical new design and announcing an improved version of the CA, with single screen, for the light van market. A hundred of the new vans were sent by rail to Martin Walter of Folkestone to produce the latest versions of the Dormobile, Dormobile Caravan and Utilecom. Martin Walter were also producing the latest versions of luxury PA estate cars. The name Dormobile itself, managed to pass into general usage as a generic name for motor caravans in much the way that most vacuum cleaners were known as Hoovers.

Both FA and PA were offered in estate versions. Here we see the PA and occupants taking time out of the car to enjoy the sunshine and read their map. (Vauxhall Motors)

This fleet of new estates outside Coaches & Components in Hatherley Road, London, are destined for the Piccadilly cigarette company's reps, or travellers as they used to be called. (Vauxhall Motors)

Though popular with driving schools and women, the Victor was aimed at the average family, as we can see from this March/April 1957 promotional edition of *Vauxhall Motorist*'s front cover. (Vauxhall Motors)

The sheer luxury of the PA Velox/Cresta estate version stand sout in this scene at Covent Garden Market *c.*1958. (Vauxhall Motors)

A Freight liner with some of its cargo, a Vauxhall Victor, at Luton Airport in 1958. (Vauxhall Motors)

New Vauxhall PAs and FAs posed near the Luton slip road of the soon to be opened MI north–south motorway in 1958. The new road was going to be the start of a programme to free British roads from congestion and make road transport even more attractive. (Vauxhall Motors)

Frank Ford remembers:

'Another difficulty with the PA was when taking bodies for Martin Walter estate conversions, without their back end body. They were driven down to Folkestone and because the petrol tanks would be replaced behind the back seat for estates, the filler came quite high up at the back. Because Walters fitted their own fillers, they were sent down with a temporary wooden bung instead of a proper cap. The drivers could not understand why they kept running out of fuel half way down when they had always been filled up. Investigations revealed that because the bung had no air vent, the tank impounded as the fuel level dropped.'

Another interesting Velox/Cresta conversion was available from Friary Motors Ltd, an associate company of Abbots of Farnham. The model was described by them, thus:

'A Six for the Space-man... No less than 52cu.ft on a flat platform big enough for two to sleep on, all steel integral, safety glass all round, seating capacity retained by automatic catches etc., even with the back seat up there is 48in load platform and 1½in more rear headroom than standard saloons.'

The motorway age would create demand for ever more powerful police cars to trap the miscreant motorists, not that these chaps and their two new Pas and one FA would see too much of motorway life on their Inverness Constabulary duties, but the cars would ensure good service, enabling Vauxhall to establish its reputation as the preferred choice of many forces. Those were the days before police cars earned the nickname 'jam sandwiches'. The cars looked rather intimidating but also reassuring to law abiding folk. (Vauxhall Motors)

Home market prices for the Velox version was £1,222 5s 10d (£360 tax)and £923 10s for the Cresta (£386 tax).

The late 1950s began the era of cheap ferry travel with punters being encouraged to 'Take your car to Norway, nowhere will you find more magnificent scenery... take your car in order that you may really discover Norway, it costs very little.' Rates were from only £5 per car, crossing from Newcastle to Bergen or Stavanger and it took less than twenty hours on the Bergen Line ships *Leda* or *Venus*. Air travel was also getting cheaper. By mid-December, all Vauxhall car deliveries to Northern Ireland went by air, using British Freight Liner which left Luton Airport daily, carrying three Victors or two PAs, plus 4,000lb of spare parts. There was strong growth in consumer spending toward the end of the 1950s, approaching £1,005 million per year by 1958, mostly paid for on hire purchase and mail order. There was a pre-election boom, enabling Prime Minister Harold MacMillan to boast in the run up to the 1959 election that the people had 'never had it so good.'

A cute little CA tipper, made possible by the chassis' versatile design. The CA was also popular as a milk float, particularly in rural areas. (Vauxhall Motors)

The famous radio doctor and Luton MP Dr Charles Hill drove the 2 millionth Vauxhall off the production line in April 1959. The left-hand-drive Cresta was destined for Canada. Significantly it had taken forty-seven years to reach the 1 million output mark and only 8½ years to reach the next million. By the end of 1959, the company was approaching the quarter millionth Vauxhall Victor, *Vauxhall Motorist* remarking that there were now enough Victors:

'to fill, nose to tail, the whole length of every one of the six lanes of the new motorway and every one of the next forty miles of similar road to be built as well. And that number of Victors has been built in under three years.'

Just prior to the M1 motorway opening, a full range of Victors, Crestas and Velox cars were photographed near the Luton A6 slip road, an image redolent of the longed for state of total freedom and style on the open road. The M1 was going to be an answer to the nation's prayers for truly happy motoring. Sadly, the Government was deciding to slash the railways at the same time, so life on the road was not going to turn out quite like that.

Vauxhall Bedford News reported in May 1959:

'A gay day indeed for road transport was Budget Day this year. The encouragement of the new investment allowances; the reduction of purchase tax on cars – a major help indeed to the many firms that run car fleets and, above all, the long awaited removal of that senseless purchase tax on commercial vehicles…'

The trade magazine went on to describe the outlook as bright, with 1958 having been a period of consolidation – Vauxhall Bedford having experienced a net trading loss of £1,134,744 in 1958. By 1959, the vast expansion programme led to a new high in car and truck sales and a net profit of £755,929. The budget was expected to give much impetus to truck demand and the car plant was working at peak capacity.

Not surprisingly, especially due to the North American market taking 59,300, Vauxhall production figures for 1959 were up 41 per cent from 174,616 to 246,085, with exports up 30 per cent to 134,912 units (55 per cent of sales). In spite of its relatively small population, Canada took 34,400 – a 131 per cent increase. The home market also grew by 55 per cent over 1958 and on 3 December 1959, the 50,000th truck left the Dunstable factory. On 31 December 1959, Martin Walter built the 10,000th Bedford Special, a four berth Dormobile on the new long (90in) wheel-base van – it was a foot longer than its predecessor. At that time the firm were producing 200 a week (managing 8,804 conversions in 1959), hoping to raise output to 300 a week in 1960. The 12-seater utilabrake achieved the largest sales. Dunstable's factory was closed for two weeks to get the new tooling ready. There was also demand for ambulances and the 12-seater PSV had been introduced in 1958. In 1959, vehicle registrations reached a record level of 1,253,002, of these 645,617 were cars. Since 1955, traffic on trunk and class one roads had increased by 50 per cent. Total CA production, starting in 1959, had reached 139,000 by 1959.

London's evening papers all used Bedford CAs in the frantic rush to deliver the capital's news. Papers were rolling off the presses ten times day, shot through hatches to crowds of men waiting in the yard ready to load up and drive off to street corner salesmen, railway stations and newsagents. The *News* had 129 CAs, Star 85 and the Standard 25. The latter hiring from United Services Transport Co. Ltd. All vans covered fifty–fifty-six miles daily, in heavy traffic and were a great advertisement for Bedford. Management and shareholders could look back on 1959 with satisfaction at record sales on a turnover of £130 million and net profit of £6,427,892 . Exports were up 30 per cent and workers benefited with shares in a profit sharing payout of £3.75 million.

There was still room for improvement on the PA and FA series and lucky Frank Ford took a team out through Germany and some Alpine passes in July 1960. He said:

'We took three cars out, one standard, one with Borg Warner overdrive and the first disc brakes ever tried and the other was standard except for two speed automatic transmission. The latter was a system known as power divide. The cars were smothered in sensors –

Women drivers were still a rarity, but this young lady is having no trouble using the controls of the very user friendly new PA Vauxhall on the increasingly congested streets of London. (Vauxhall Motors)

bi-metal thermocouples – to check temperatures. It was great fun going abroad. I tested the improved Victor, the FB, in Grenada, taking daily runs along a figure-of-eight route through orange groves in the foothills of the Sierra Nevada in January.'

In February 1960, a special overseas version of the Victor was announced, called the Envoy. Built at Luton, along with the Victor, Victor Super, Victor de luxe and

A first series FA Victor, very popular with lady drivers but Vauxhall engineer Frank Ford had to teach one man how to apply the brakes in his wife's FA! (Vauxhall Motors)

the estate car, there were differences in trim and a special selection of bright attractive colours and a white wall tyres option. Standard items included laminated windscreen, heater and de mister, and oil bath air cleaner.

With so many new owners taking pride in their new cars, Vauxhall offered a scheme called the Owners Protection Policy. It offered more even spreading of service charges over the vehicle's mileage, longer intervals between services (2,000 instead of 1,000, made possible by improved efficiency and durability of parts) and time interval servicing when mileage built up slowly. Vauxhall also continued to advertise their 'short motor' units, avoiding the cost of a new engine and available for a range of models.

Vauxhall have always known the importance of good customer relations and Frank Ford was moved on to the role of external contract engineer, travelling around the country with a man from the service department. This was good for customer relations and keeping track of production car frailties. He said:

'Any problems that occurred we wanted to know about, fix and get on to the production cars as soon as possible. There were four of us on the job, two covering cars and two on trucks. I recall a few interesting episodes, like curing a clutch slip by changing the carburettor on a PB Cresta in Plymouth. This retired chap's bungalow was in an extremely good spot overlooking the River Tamar. The trouble was that it was set a long way down the slope of an extremely steep gradient and he had to reverse up to get out. In so doing he had burned out two clutches in 3,000 miles. I got the briefing from the service department of Allen's in Plymouth. Their basement workshop had a ramp up into the showroom of similar gradient to the customer's. I tried reversing up with the clutch fully engaged and it wouldn't go. After a night's sleep I realised that as I pulled away in reverse there was bound to be a bit of a jerk and this force would pull fuel away from the jets. Having spotted a newer model in the showroom, fitted with a bigger carb, I asked the fitter to swop them. With this modification, the car reversed up the slope like a bird taking flight, no need to slip the clutch. That was the only time I ever received a letter of thanks from a customer via the service manager. Customers weren't always polite. A man down in Dorking said his wife's car brakes didn't work properly. He was quite stroppy. We had a pressometer which was a pressure gauge that could be fitted over the brake pedal to measure how hard someone was pressing. We went down to see this chap. With the service manager and the customer, who drove, we went onto the A25 Dorking - Redhill - Reigate road. I told him to brake as fast as he could, and we just came slowly to a stop. I asked him to let me try and we came to a halt in a cloud of his tyre rubber. When he asked me how I did it, I said 'with the brake'. I used the pressometer to show him the difference between what we had done to stop his car. Then I said, 'when you get back home adjust the seat so that your leg is not quite straight, then when you brake you'll get more pressure as you straighten your leg.' Customer education was a big part of that job. We were like the Gods from Mount Olympus, the last resort in dealing with a problem. It was a very nice feeling to come away from a satisfied customer who might buy another Vauxhall.'

Satisfied customers there were in plenty. In April 1960, *Vauxhall Motorist* posed the question:

'Ever noticed how many Victors bearing driving school plates you see on the road. The reason is obvious enough of course – the Victor is one of the easiest cars to drive there's ever been, and the schools were quick to cash in on the fact.'

The British School of Motoring (BSM) were among fleet users. Miss Denise McCann took over as chairman and managing director of BSM in 1953. She was one of the best-known members of the Institute of Directors, and an influential and valued customer of the motor industry. Running her own interior decorating business led to a contract helping rebuild BSM's war damaged offices, and on to a role as assistant MD. She became chairman and chief executive when founder S.C.H. Roberts died. The *Vauxhall Motorist* reporter observed in July 1973:

'She is a confident and altogether unladylike driver of startlingly fast cars – Ferraris, Aston Martins, Porches and her personal Rolls Royce Corniche. Therefore it is not surprising that she established a trend for BSM to use Vauxhalls.'

Even more production capacity was going to be required to keep up with demand. Luton had become something of a boom town at the start of the 1960s. Roger Wash recalls that Luton had something of the atmosphere of 'Dodge City' in the early 1960s as newcomers flocked in to take their chance in a booming local economy at which Vauxhall Bedford Motors were at the centre. Irishman John Cheevers said:

> 'There were lots of nationalities, and a lot of prejudice against the Irish, but we learned to get along with each other. Although it was shift work there was a lot of camaraderie. Working for the Yanks you could be sure of a good pension.'

The boom was something of an illusion, as the UK's balance of payments worsening quickly after the Tory victory owing to excessive imports, and would have been much worse without the best efforts of successful companies like Vauxhall. The trade deficit on visible trade approached £408 million in 1960, not auguring well for much needed road improvements. Spending dipped briefly, but Prime Minister Macmillan, having claimed that the luxuries of the rich had become the necessities of the poor, would have to go along with it.

Vauxhall would have to be wary of the kind of industrial unrest that could come from any government efforts toward wage restraint. Management continued in positive vein. Motoring had never been more popular, so much so in fact that a government report on manufacturers in 1963 said, 'The population appears as intent upon owning cars as manufacturers are upon meeting demand'. The 1960s would see the nation's car owners double in number from 5.6 million to 11.8 million. Style was the key to 1960s living and by 1963 Vauxhall would have a Styling Centre to be proud of, even if some architecture critics disapproved. Disapproval from the establishment was essential to the 'get with it' generation. Getting with it in technology terms was more challenging for car makers. The BMC mini was the darling of the age. Vauxhall had to find a competitor.

CHAPTER EIGHT

VIVA VAUXHALL

In the truck market the company were already ahead of the field, launching the radically different TK range, including two tonners and 12-ton tractor units, in 1960. Worldwide demand for Bedfords was long established. In his twenties Reg Condon drove Bedfords in Australia for William Angliss Meats, in the early 1950s, Reg said;

'I drove a 1948 Bedford interstate, delivering small goods as the trucks then weren't refrigerated. It had a four speed gear box with a splitter (dividing the box between high and low ranges), a bit slow, only capable of about 80kph, sluggish and gutless, but very reliable and never broke down, they were a very good engine.

The engine was in the cabin next to the driver so it got hot and extremely uncomfortable. The only trouble was when you lost a tyre. I liked the Bedfords. Interestingly, at the time of writing, Loys soft drinks company, who deliver discount drinks to customers' doors in the Melbourne area, were still using a 1971 Bedford.

Like Australia, Nigeria was building its own Bedfords, such was demand. Clearly West Africa was going to play an increasing part in the world scene and there would be much work for Bedfords. The United Africa Company (UAC) were distributors of Vauxhall cars and Bedford trucks for the whole Commonwealth and a £310,000 investment in a CKD assembly plant would save much on shipping space and cost. Personnel were sent over to Dunstable for training.

By January 1960 the Bedford R type four wheel drive was fitted with the 97 bhp Bedford 300cu.in diesel alternative to petrol. This rugged truck was popular with public utilities like the GPO and British Waterways. The British Army also continued as a main customer. Bedford tippers and various conversion options for seven tonners were also as popular as ever. Bedford developments that year also included the half-ton Vauxhall-engined pick up and a two speed axle available on the Bedford passenger chassis.

Then came the quantum leap forward with the announcement of the TK Bedford, replacing the famed forward control S type and to meet four basic design criteria: safety, speed of action, crew comfort and elimination of driver fatigue.

Four new British Overseas Airways Corporation Bedord SB coaches flank and Bedford CA van, at Heathrow in the early 1950s. One of the state owned airlines new Bristol Britannia turbo prop airliners completes this image of modernising Britain. (Vauxhall Motors)

Bedford S type. This Dutch registered vehicle was photographed at the Cambridge Bedford Gathering of August 2003. (Robert Cook)

A Study in Contrasts

The latest means of transport being landed in the same old primitive way at Accra, Gold Coast. Two surf boats are lashed together and paddled by natives to the beach. The photograph was sent to us by a reader.

A Vauxhall car arriving at its destination on Africa's Gold Coast during the early 1930s. (Vauxhall Motors)

In the words of *Vauxhall – Bedford News*:

> 'In more ways than one, they put the driver out in front... The TK Bedford marks a leap forward in truck design that has no equal precedent.'

The model was demonstrated to press, fleet operators and big groups of dealers in July and August. Specifications included:

1) Completely new cab ahead of engine layout.
2) Low step entry to cab that's like a car for comfort.
3) Easy two side access to separate engine compartment.
4) Road visibility up to 7½ feet from cab.
5) High efficiency brakes with multiple safety features – light touch and fade resistant.
6) 16in low-level load wheels right up to 5-tonners.
7) Comprehensive payload cover from 3 tons up to 12 tons.

The engine, a proven Bedford diesel or petrol unit, was placed vertically in an entirely separate compartment at the rear of the cab. Routine maintenance and even removal of the cylinder head was simplified.

Some S types and the four wheel drive R types are still in service. The types proved popular with fire brigades across Britain and have been retained by the cost constrained armed forces, infamously known as Green Godesses. This picture was taken in Northampton during the 2002 fireman's strike when once again they were pressed into civilian service. (Robert Cook)

The rugged so-called 'Big Bedford' R (four-wheel drive) type always looked at home in the more exotic African environment as we see here in the 1960s. (Vauxhall Motors)

One of the new TK Bedfords on the final assembly line, August 1960, at Dunstable. (Vauxhall Motors)

Modern Transport magazine wrote, in September 1960:

> 'The TK range represents a bold, and we think successful attack on the inadequacies and disadvantages of the forward control configuration while retaining all the advantages and achieving quite exceptional good looks.'

The basic truck cost £1,280 and production continued alongside the R type and normal control vehicles for the time being.

The early 1960s were extremely optimistic. It is the Year Zero mentality; traffic growth and hectic haulage were seen as positive signs, and traffic wardens made their first appearance in London. Vauxhall were well into the swing of the expansive outlook gripping Britain announcing further building projects at Luton and Ellesmere Port. A former RAF camp, Hooton Park, on the south bank of the Mersey was chosen. Vauxhall's chairman and MD, Phillip Copelin, announced that since 1958 it had become clear that further growth was needed to meet rising demand. For economic and social reasons he would have preferred to expand Luton and Dunstable but after discussion with the Board of Trade it was felt that the company should adapt its plans to Government policy of steering development to areas of under-employment.

A 1976 Bedford TK still delivering coal around Buckingham and villages in March 1999. (Robert Cook)

A preserved 1968 KM with impressive twin headlamps at the Bedford Gathering in August 2003. (Robert Cook)

The TL, this registration MCV 263X, was some improvement on the TK. This one was still in regular use on runs from Newlyn Harbour when photographed in July 2003. (Robert Cook)

Thirty possible sites had been visited by directors. They sought a location suitable for current and predicted needs, close to all types of manpower, technical and educational services, good sea and rail access, closer to supplies, markets and the Luton and Dunstable sites. The hoped to create new plant to include manufacture of the full range of Bedford trucks and light vans on a 2.5 million square foot area, employing 7,000. Development work would proceed in two stages. Stage one would involve building a press shop, body build shop, with paint, trim and final assembly facilities for commercials. Taking over two years to complete, Vauxhall Bedford Motors expected it to cost £30 million, employ 3,500, increasing capacity to 100,000 units a year. The bulldozers moved into Hooton Park in August 1961. By November 1962, the first production machinery would be cranking out components.

Work would involve developing the site into a fully integrated commercial vehicle plant, adding buildings and plant for engines, axles and gearboxes which would be transferred from the Bedford factory in Dunstable. Space created would be available for more car making in the Luton Dunstable area. Total company strength would reach 34,000. The Luton plant would also get a new building for style, design and product engineering.

Inevitably, where so much machinery and heavyweight materials are involved, there will be some serious accidents. Plans also allowed for new medical and rehabilitation facilities were also included in the scheme to free space at the Luton plant. Freda Eastlake was one of the first nursing staff helping to rehabilitate

Vauxhall's new styling centre in Osborne Road, Luton, very much a design of the age and redolent of London's infamous Centre Point. (Vauxhall Motors)

injured employees. Whether employees were hurt at or away from work, Vauxhall's scheme was designed to help them back toward earning a living – the scheme was very beneficial to those disabled by the war. Mrs Eastlake said this was very important during the early post-war years when state benefits were minimal. She said that the company worked closely with a consultant at the local Luton and Dunstable Hospital. A company publication, *The Road Back*, published in the early 1960s, offers some thought-provoking examples of what was achieved. The booklet explained:

'The traditional approach to the treatment of a disabled worker in industry favours keeping him off work until recovery has taken place. If he is left handicapped, industry does not always find it easy or convenient to re absorb him.'

Vauxhall gave examples ranging from a broken back to a man suffering from a 'dropped wrist', which while:

'not necessarily an industrial accident, can happen from nerve palsy due to prolonged pressure. The springs of the lightweight perspex splint made in the retraining shop do the work of the immobilised muscles and can be used while normal occupations are followed.'

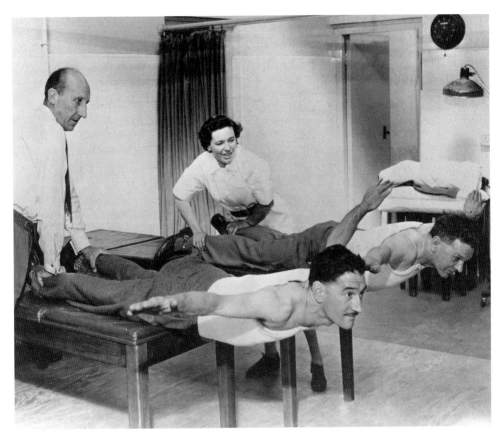

Freda Eastlake at work in the rehabilitation unit, early 1950s. (Vauxhall Motors)

Company literature commented:

> 'Enlightened management, by providing facilities such as these, can make an important contribution to medicine, to the individual and to the State. Among teachers of medicine and the allied professions, no less than in industry, a wider recognition of the value and possibilities of modern rehabilitation is already apparent. Centres of this kind may provide a prototype for future development on an ever widening scale.'

Making the most of resources, material and human were watchwords for management. Vauxhall entered 1961 offering variety in detail and model colour, but with no price increase for six-cylinder models which now included a venetian blind over the rear window. Hydramatic transmission was now tried and tested, being announced as brand new in October 1960 and now an option. *Vauxhall Motorist* described the new system thus:

> 'A kind of driving that's very different, that calls for still less effort from the driver; that brings new smoothness, new pleasure, new efficiency. And that still leaves the driver in full control.'

The sporty Vauxhall Cresta, in its element on a continental rally, winter 1960. (Vauxhall Motors)

Paul Frere, a Belgian racing driver and motoring writer, considered the hydramatic gear box:

> 'Very lively with the new engine... good and very smooth. I like the kick down to first at 30mph – you can really use low gear.'

Advertising material explained that with this automatic system you might not notice the gear change which was always at the right moment and beautifully

The PA Cresta and Velox was equally at home around the capital and could, in the right colours, look most regal. (Vauxhall Motors)

smooth. It worked, and still does, on the principle of a fluid coupling. Oil pressure is controlled by the throttle valve. Rather like two fans, one electric driven, the other freewheeling. The powered fan blows air against the blades of the freewheeler causing it to rotate. Imagine oil jetting instead of air, turning a plate attached to a prop shaft which turns the road wheels. Transmission oil was carefully developed and the system could adjust for reverse, as well as offering a mesh with large or small cogs to allow two variable gear ratios. Simple, but brilliant, and not new to the vast world of General Motors.

Cars Illustrated wrote:

'There is minimum fatigue and consequent lessening of frustration – both hands are free for steering the car – and there is no doubt that this form of transmission is ideal for day-to-day motoring and for the not so expert and yet the enthusiast will enjoy driving it too. Undoubtedly the smoothest Vauxhall yet.

A Hydramatic Velox cost £1,099 0s 10d (including £324 purchase tax) and the Cresta version cost £1,284. The hydramatic Velox also proved itself in that year's Mobil Economy run, achieving an average of 29.2mpg over the three-day, 1,000-mile course. The cars also featured new sealed-beam lights commensurate with the motorway age. Carreras were so impressed that they chose the Friary estate version of their Picadilly cigarette travellers – conversion of the basic saloon to a Friary was a mere £200. Victor estates were popular with cigarette makers Rothmans for their Peter Stuyvesant reps. The whole concept of 'estate cars' reflected the still quaintly old fashioned elements of 1960s Britain and a strong market orientation for Vauxhall. Even the Queen was supplied with a Friary PA Cresta conversion.

Autocar compared the 1961 Velox and Cresta with the previous year's models. Both were fitted with Laycock-de-Normanville overdrive, available for £64 extra plus tax, taking the Velox price up to £1,077 15s 10d with tax. *Autocar* reported:

> 'An overdrive of this type, with instantaneous engagement or disenagement by an electric tumble switch, is especially useful in city traffic when everything except restarts from rest can be accomplished in second and overdrive second.'

The magazine also noted that the low rate suspension gave unusually level and well-damped ride, not jolting passengers when riding over the many pot holes on British roads. The brakes were also judged impressive, using larger front drums to achieve maximum deceleration of 0.95g to pull up dead square without locking the brakes – front wheel discs were an optional extra. There were fifteen colour choices, all employing the benefits of Vauxhall Stresscoat resting to minimise paint cracking through driving stresses, thus reducing rusting rates.

In, 1961, the year of the first MoT tests and Bedford's 100,000th truck (January), 'Sixes' (The PASX) received a bigger 2.6 litre, in-line engine of square design and 3.25 bore and stroke. Gearbox ratios were unchanged while the rear axle ratio changed from 4.11:1 to 3.90:1. Wheels were bigger, at 5.90 x 14 but tyre revolutions per mile were the same. A bigger engine reduced rpm, but the bigger engine required a bigger clutch (nine inches) and massive new rubber-cushioned engine mountings. The cars also benefited further from the option of power-assisted braking, a sensible choice given the rising speeds coming from engines developed at the company's Chaul End engine and transmission research facility. Power assistance was provided by hydraulic and vacuum servo units mounted on the offside of the engine. These could be fitted to post-1957 cars for £2 17s 6d, in two hours.

The Vauxhall Victor, costing £723 12s 2d, was updated, creating an instrument cluster, featuring a bold red speedometer needle with a 7.25in arc covering 0-90mph, was almost as wide as the steering wheel. The estate car, which cost £858 4s 2d including tax, had increased load capacity and steel shell big end bearings. The *Vauxhall Motorist* produced a retrospect on the Victor in October 1961, confident that it was sure to be the used car choice of many. Hard to beat on economy,as the 1961 Mobil Economy run attested when a Victor averaged 40.39mpg. Introduced in 1957, 400,000 were built in 4½ years and exported to eighty-two different countries, with Canada taking the most – 81,000. A Victor was also in Simons' taxi service on Alderney in the Channel Islands. They had used Vauxhalls for years, boasting a 1954 Velox that had travelled 84,000 miles over roads mainly of rough cobbles – the island having only thirty miles properly surfaced in 1961.

The FB Victor showed a new approach to styling, with a light, tough body shell, box girder framework, stressed sheet metal skin. The 1,508cc engine was similar to the MKI's but more powerful and quieter, producing 56.33bhp at 4,600rpm and 85.6bhp at 2,200rpm, compared to 54.8bhp and 84.5bhp on the old model. There was now a choice of fourteen different colours. Better materials and sealing meant only two nipples on the near side front suspension ball joints and two off side needed five minutes lubrication every 12,000 miles and engine oil change every 2-3000 miles. By today's standards this was still a lot of work but a great labour saving situation in 1961. Soon the world of little niggardly problems for readers to write into the *Vauxhall Motorist* would, like the magazine, be gone. For now, however, life on the readers' pages were as charming as ever, with one such advising drivers to add a dessert-spoonful of Lux to the screen wash as it did wonders for his 1959 Cresta while Mr Millins of the Isle of Wight sent in a picture of his Cresta and trailer on thatching duties around the island

In April 1961, William Swallow succeeded Phillip Copelin as MD. The latter transferred to become Manager of New York staff of GM's overseas operations. Copelin had arrived at Vauxhall from AC Sphinx (later AC Delco). He had seen vehicle output grow from 143,000 in 1955 to 252,000 in 1960 and payroll growth from £11 million per year to £25 million. Production developments had to keep pace with new model development. Assembling shock absorbers was one example of how labour was being used intensively in the early 1960s. The piston unit, being made up of so many small light pieces – the eleven rings and washers, shims, etc., had to be fitted onto a rod and it was difficult to create a machine to do the job. Vauxhall overcame the problem, designing their own equipment that could complete 600 units an hour. This consisted of a circular table with twelve assembly heads evenly spaced around the edge, feeding itself automatically; taking the rods, dropping them into holders and then selecting each of eleven other small pieces – some of them only .007in thick – fed from vibratory hoppers or mechanical pick-off arms. It assembled these onto the rods the correct way up, in the proper sequence, finishing off by tightening a nut on the threaded end of the rod and tightening it to a pre-set torque.

Modern machinery was also helping engine production. Six-cylinder units were built on a pedestal type conveyor in 1962, while Victor engines continued being assembled on the earlier type of bench level slat conveyor. Segregation of four- and six-cylinder assembly allowed for the increase in four-cylinder production needed to meet the strong demand for the latest Victors

The new sporty VX 4/90 version was introduced toward the end of the year, described as 'The car for the man who wants a bit more...'. Still basically a Victor, improvements principal improvements were: a new four speed synchromesh gearbox, aluminium high compression cylinder head (painted red) giving 44 per cent more power at 81 gross bhp, twin Zenith carburettors, Lockheed 10.5in disc

Launching the new FB Victor at a London venue for VIPs and journalists to enjoy and spread the word. (Vauxhall Motors)

brakes, six clearly visible dashboard dials, short gear shift and a luxurious interior. *Autocar* commented: '...we agreed that Vauxhall deserve equal congratulation for the latest Victor which has become the style leader among the British one and a halfs... This new car looks right from every angle.' The snooty *Guardian* called the VX: 'a medium priced saloon of merit. Vauxhall also followed up with a new safety belt combining lap and diagonal, with special anchorage for this high performance car. It cost £4 4s 0d.

October 1962's *Vauxhall Motorist* cover showed the smart new PB version of Cresta, another credit to the styling department, though perhaps appearing a trifle cumbersome alongside the new Rover 2000, soon to emerge as a competitor. Once again the US influence on the Vauxhall Sixes was obvious. The car looked something like an enlarged FB Victor, though US-style influence was still evident. The magazine's editorial carried a feature the styling department in December 1962, suggesting that it looked like a prison compound, being a high-walled pen in the middle of the factory, with a locked gate to keep the secrets in and the spies out.' In this austere roofless pen the new models were seen for the first time. Of the pen's inmates, the magazine opined:

'Here come the silent, rather withdrawn men of the styling division to reveal their treasured secret to the 'top people' in the company concerned with model development.'

Vauxhall continued to favour the country set with a most useful estate version, a type also very convenient for anyone going on holiday and for commercial travellers. This young lady also seems to be demonstrating the time honoured possibilities of using the large luggage space for overnight resting. (Vauxhall Motors)

The process of creating a new model started with the Product Policy Group, representing manufacturing, supply, finance, engineering and styling. Over a period of six months they would decide on the broad specification, size, weight, price, class and introduction date. Work then started with colour diagrammatic drawings, clay and glass fibre models. The first ten days were about floating ideas, with drawings. Full-size drawings of front, rear and sides were produced on wall mounted drawing surfaces. Checks were made to ensure that mechanics matched the design and that the design could be translated into sheet metal work. A full size model was then produced by applying two inches of clay to a wooden frame, with all-important seating buck included. The stylist's clay contained a beeswax base, pigmented and toughened with fillers, It was stored in an oven to keep it malleable at room temperature.

The clay model received two viewing for suggestions. Seating was checked for entry and exit and then it was sent to the glass fibre shop, where panels were made in plaster moulds. Painted panels were assembled, creating a model accurate in every detail. Even the instrument panel was there. As *Vauxhall Motorist* observed:

32me RALLYE AUTOMOBILE MONTE-CARLO 1963

PHOTO SOLEIL A VILLEFRANCHE-SUR-MER ET STUDIO PELISSIER 13 BIS RUE TRACHEL NICE

There is nothing restful about this image as the Victor VX 4/90 shows its colours in the 1963 Monte Carlo Rally. (Vauxhall Motors)

'A new car is not an all-male design any more than it is an all-male possession.' The writer went on to explain that women were the key influence on interior finish. The prototype was then tested and it was on to release and Earls' Court Motor Show.

The continuing quest for better cars required parallel efforts to keep production facilities in step. Thus, early in 1963 a 250,000sq.ft extension of Ellesmere Port was announced by William Swallow and Luton MP Rt Hon. Dr Charles Hill laid a foundation stone for the office block. Mr Swallow said that the 1,235,000sq.ft factory would be in full operation by the second half of the year. Limited component production was already under way and employees were expected to reach 3,000-3,500 by the end of 1963, all being local except for 250 supervisors from Luton and Dunstable. Another milestone was reached that year with the retirement of Deputy Chairman Reg Pearson OBE, after ten years in office. Sir Reginald had risen from fitter and turner in 1919, when the company was employing a mere 1,000 workers, (by 1963 the figure had reached 25,000), to foreman, area manager, assistant production manager and works manager before joining the board in 1946. He had played a key role in good labour relations, training apprentices and employee welfare.

A new design at the clay model stage in the 1970s. (Vauxhall Motors)

This was also the year that Dr Richard Beeching, chairman of British Railways, announced savage line cuts to help cover £160 million annual losses. He was encouraged by road builder and transport Minister Ernest Marples who wanted even more cuts. There was no thought toward a balanced and integrated transport system, just a short-term solution. Although the massive new flyovers were rising to carry the M4 motorway into London, hot on the heels of the M1's success, new road plans still lacked behind any serious calculations of traffic volume growth – for all the bluster, 600 miles of motorway had been built by 1969. *Vauxhall Motorist* carried an article in June 1963, on the wisdom of turning railways into roads. Moreover, large rural areas lost rail routes and little was done to boost an alternative bus network. The void would have to be filled by the car. Meanwhile Britain's world trade position worsened as the spending boom eventually had to be paid for and labour relations issues confronted.

Labour relations in Luton were so good in the early 1960s that sociologists Goldthorpe, Lockwood *et al* visited the town to test the thesis that the working classes were becoming embourgeoised (more like the middle class in their life style) because they were earning such high wages. They looked at 229 workers and at a comparative group of fifty-four white collar staff from Vauxhall, Laporte and Skefko Ball Bearings. They concluded that the working man's social world

A BOAC Bedford SB coach waits alongside a steam train at Paddington station in the 1950s, but railways were running out of steam in more ways than one! (Vauxhall Motors)

was much more limited to his family and that the new workers, having migrated from afar, lacked even the community of the more traditional working class of older industries.

Such comparisons seem irrelevant now, the old social structures having changed irrevocably, some might say disintegrated. Did neglect of old industries and capitalism's greed to exploit new high profit industries wreck the old communities and overload places like Luton? Is the car a curse that we cannot get rid of? Was it the lure of high pay from company's like Vauxhall and the glamorous car, or was the desire for cars and other luxury goods merely the expression of the masses' desire for freedom and some sort of equality? Does it matter and can any of the accidents of history be put into some kind of neat theory? One thing just leads to another and the car industry was playing a vital part in the export drive, filling gaps in a crumbling public transport system at home and paying lots of tax. Bedford coaches, and their long partnership with bodybuilders Duple, was also doing its bit for PSV and touring. Coach travel, however, was not going to restrain the freedom-loving motorist. Early in 1964, British Rail announced that they expected to ferry 500,000 cars across the channel, nearly 200,000 more than the 1963 record.

Two HA Vivas, a couple of golden oldies and four rather important and sober looking chaps pose at Vauxhall's Osborne Road premises, the Styling Centre rises up in the background as Vauxhall prepares to enter the 'swinging sixties. (Vauxhall Motors)

The company was on the right course, with new designs looking rather more British and less rust prone. Vauxhall Bedford announced net profits of £5,975,955 in 1962 compared with £4,328,923 in 1961, on a turnover of £126 million – an increase of 7 per cent. The profit-sharing scheme paid out £388,000, equalling £17 2s 6d, before tax, for each employee – Vauxhall had paid out nearly £5 million in twenty-eight years. Total vehicle sales were up by 16 per cent at 215,974 vehicles, an increase of 77 per cent on the home market which had much to do with Britain's easy credit. Exports accounted for 111,930 vehicles, or 52 per cent of total sales; valued at £60 million. With justified optimism, another £13.8 million was spent on new plant and tooling, mostly at Ellesmere Port which had started producing components and sub-assemblies for Luton and Dunstable.

In this milieu, the Victor and VX 4/90 variant were in steady demand, on sale for £634 9s and £840 7s 1d (including tax) respectively, with the latter cutting a dash in the sports world, but no rival to the Lotus Cortina across country. Bill Blydenstein had some success racing the VX 4/90 in the 1,600cc class, but could not match the Italian factories. Vauxhall needed something else and it was on the way. In October 1963 *Vauxhall Motorist* proudly displayed their latest model, with the caption: 'Viva, designed with you in mind. This all new Viva has fine clean lines, real good looks like all other Vauxhalls of today.' The first models, the HA and HA90 had 44bhp and 60bhp engines respectively and four speed all synchromesh gear box. Born in the BMC Mini's heyday, it faces serious competition and was not so sexy, iconic or compatible with the age of the mini skirt. It was quite a square looking car.

The car would have to be judged on its merits and value for money. The Morris Mini Minor, also badged as Austin Seven, had appeared in 1959, a masterpiece of engineering setting a trend for others to follow. Designer Alec Issigonis had designed it on the back of a cigarette packet, placing the engine sideways to drive the front wheels and save on length. It was unique, held the road like a go–cart and gained three wins in the Monte Carlo Rally. Rally drivers could handle the gears as if it was an automatic, listening to the revs to gear change without the time-wasting clutch. It would be a hard act to compete with in the small car market, let alone on the race track. Vauxhall had to re-connect with its racing past. The unassuming little Viva would lead the way

The first edition in September 1963 seemed an unlikely contender for glory. The best that could be said at first sight was that this was a car offering economy, good basic performance, comfort and reliability, in two- or four-door versions. It was no technical breakthrough into the unorthodox. It was just the product of well-tried engineering practice, offering better value for money than buyers would get from anything else in its class. *Vauxhall Motorist* noted: 'As with all Vauxhalls, ornamentation is restrained...' The car made clever use of window glass to create an interior width of 51in in a body of only 58.5in. Overall length was 12ft 11in on a 7ft 7in wheelbase. The 1,057cc OV engine, with chain driven camshaft, was completely new. *Vauxhall Motorist's* assessment included:

> 'Perhaps the most important of all features of the Viva is its background, the continuous process of engineering evaluation that has enabled Vauxhall to offer the car buying world better cars representing better value for money.'

Investment in Ellesmere Port and Luton had happened with the Viva in mind. The new plant's 320ft assembly conveyor was fed from various component lines, and was capable of fifty units per day to within very fine limits of accuracy.

Starting with part assembly at the new plant, whole car assembly shifted to Ellesmere Port, the first HA rolling of the new production line on 1 June 1964. Enjoying the local connection and much needed regional job boost, the *Liverpool Daily Post* described the Viva as: 'For safe fast driving over any route, I do not think the beautifully balanced Viva can be matched... in its class.'

Geoffrey Charles of *The Times* wrote, 'Much common-sense planning has gone into the Viva... a rugged, practical car, competitively priced.' *Motor Transport* magazine, October 1963, said that, 'The Vauxhall Viva has everything in its favour for establishing itself as one of the most successful fleet cars ever produced.'

This young lady demonstrates
how easily the HA van
version of the Viva could be
adapted, by Martin Walter,
to camping and touring.
(Vauxhall Motors)

It would live up to this accolade in both car and Bedford-badged van forms – the latter favoured by British Telecom and as the HA Dormobile camper. The *Daily Mail*'s Dennis Holmes wrote on the subject of the Viva gearbox as, '...one of the best I have ever used... the crisp four-speed gear box has tremendous driver appeal.' This box was built on a 120ft conveyor belt at Ellesmere Port, along which at one point of the ninety-minute journey, the gearbox was lifted automatically and spun against a bearing bar which machined three separate faces simultaneously.

The Vauxhall Victor also got a makeover for the 1964 season, with engine size increased from 1,508cc to 1,594cc, compression ratio rising from 8:1 to 8:5, giving an increase in power and torque from 1,500rpm to 4,800rpm, and better acceleration. Top speed went up to 80mph. Extra luxury was available in the de luxe model, including leather trimmed and individual front seats, including new arm rests with built in ash trays – all for £10 extra. Interestingly, the new Victor and PB range marked the end of the company's historic use of bonnet flutes. With all this extra power from new Vauxhalls, one *Vauxhall Motorist* reader, A. Stevens of Swindon, Wilts, felt the need to ask the editor to call for a new 60mph motorway limit. He felt the speed differentials of modern cars were becoming a problem.

Vauxhall did not see the problem. Sales figures for 1963 reached 248,227 units, 15 per cent up on 1962. British sales hit a new record of 135,690, 30 per cent up on

1962. Exports showed a slight increase to 112,537 units, 38,487 were commercials. More components were exported to India and Argentina for local manufacturing. By the end of 1963, 26,000 Vivas were built, a rate of 400 per day and half were exported. The Viva production line was front cover news for *Vauxhall Motorist* in June 1964, with the de luxe model costing £566 1s 3d, and disc brakes an optional extra.

The Viva body involved just fourteen major body pressings, translated into six main sub assemblies for the final body welds, giving greater accuracy and simplicity to production. Up to forty Viva bodies per hour were handled by three conveyors. The Victor and six-cylinder cars came off of a similar conveyor line.

Meanwhile the company had to go on looking to the future and was still consulting the workforce in the pursuit of new ideas. Since the ideas scheme was introduced in 1942, £104,000 had been paid out. In the words made famous by a supermarket advert, 'every little helps' toward completing the bigger picture. The bigger picture was ultimately read in production and sales figures. Very happily, the company could report that they had built 100,000 Vivas by July 1964, a period of just ten months. Of these 46,000 went overseas, many to Australia, where twenty-six went to work as police 'prowl' cars in Sydney, Australia. The compact length and tight steering lock made them ideal for such work. The 100,000th Viva went to Canada, the biggest single export market for the Viva. The cars were also popular with driving schools, continuing a long tradition. It was very much a case of 'Viva Vauxhall.'

CHAPTER NINE

GOOD REASON FOR PREJUDICE

Vehicles were getting better but roads were not. In 1960 total motor tax was £590 million with central Government spending on roads £111 million. Tax had risen to £786 million by 1964 but spending to only £191 million. The AA was still providing its Woman Pilot scheme to help motorists across London, which took just as long as it did ten years earlier and could be daunting. A. Steadman from London SW1 wrote to the *Vauxhall Motorist* praising an article on the need for a congestion charge in central London.

In November 1963, Government had published a report called 'Traffic in Towns'. Its theme could be summarised by the last sentence:

'recreating the urban environment in a vigorous and lively way could do more than anything to make it (Britain) the most exciting country in the world, with incalculable results for our welfare and prosperity.'

Examples of these ideas in action included demolishing the centre of Luton to replace it with a giant shopping mall and filling acres of North Bucks countryside with Milton Keynes! The age of the multi-storey car park approached, with Liverpool Council promising 21,000 such parking spaces by 1981. They most certainly did not resolve the problem of urban decay. This has something to do with politicians working on the principles of expediency and motor engineers along the lines of careful and relentless logic, Though they do not always get it right, the car buyer has had a consistently better deal than the road user.

Mark Lynch wrote a piece for the June 1964 edition of *Vauxhall Motorist*, entitled 'Account rendered'. It was his history as a user of Vauxhalls, full of interesting recollections, as follows:

'My first was a 1956 Wyvern which gave me over three years of utter dependability... in late 1959 I graduated to six cylinders with a 1960 model Cresta... Maybe not as excellent as the Wyvern... On a long continental trip that 2¼ litre Cresta gave me 31mpg, another good reason for prejudice.'

Full frontal of the FC Victor. It is a demo car and this is what it would look like in the heart of the country. It has entranced the ladies but 'dad' appears to be evaluating it in a more manly and practical way. The trick for a designer in the 'with it' 1960s was to appeal to both sexes. (Vauxhall Motors)

The Viva's performance was 57mpg, gaining it second place in the Mobil economy run for 1964. The basic car was then available for £527 7s 11d, by far the cheapest in the range – the de luxe cost £566 1s 3d. The Victor cost £634 18s 11d, Victor Super £667 11s 3d, Victor Estate £737 12s 11d, and estate de luxe £816 3s 9d. Front disc brakes for Victors cost £20 10s 10d and the four-speed gearbox £14 10s more. At the top of the range, the Cresta cost £943 1s 3d, and the Cresta Estate £1,305 11s 3d. Overdrive cost an additional £57 7s 6d and the hydramatic gearbox a further £114 15s 10d. A sales slogan of the day read, 'Let's take my car they'll be saying, if you buy a Vauxhall.' Power steering was also to become optional on the Velox and Cresta, along with super traction differentials to reduce wheel spin. One-upmanship has always been rife among motorists. On the Bedford front, Martin Walter offered the Dormobile for £665, with purchase tax abolished on commercials.

Up until 1965, Ellesmere port had been assembling cars from the mechanical units they had built, attaching them to body panels sent up by rail from Luton. With production targets increased to 200,000, Luton could not keep pace with demand. Ellesmere was to take over all the work, being developed into a unit capable of building 91,000 cars a year by 1966. The Viva was improved for 1965,

One of the best ways to advertise and prove a car's prowess was to take it on an endurance run, as we see here with the FC 101 in 1964. (Vauxhall Motors)

gaining a more efficient fuel filter system, better fuel economy, more interior and exterior colours. The steering gear ratio was raised from 3.79 to 3.14 turns lock to lock. Other details included new upholstery for the de luxe, a fitted boot mat, and arm rests in contrasting colours to match the door trim.

Luton would still have plenty to do. The new 'sixes' were introduced in 1963 and by 1965 had a reputation for smooth, powerful elegant motoring. These cars featured a new four-speed, all-synchro, floor gear change, attractive new grille and large 3.3 litre engine, along with the hydramatic option, new and two tone colours, individual or fully reclining front seats, central arm rest, headlamp flashers, cigarette lighter, and screen washer. There was further luxury with Connolly leather in the Cresta de luxe and estate car. An all-new Victor 101 (FC model) was also announced for the 1965 season, described by the makers as 'the greatest Vauxhall yet' and featuring what they called space curves. This was a reference to the creation of inner space through use of curved side panels and thinner pillars. They certainly sold well, 219,814 being produced between introduction at the end of 1964 and 1967. There was, of course, a VX 4/90 version.

The 10 millionth GM vehicle exported overseas, arrived in Antwerp in 1965. It was a silver Vauxhall Victor 101, delivered from Luton and assembled in GM's Antwerp plant.

Bedford's star was also in the ascendant, gaining the lead in world truck exports. The division moved into the heavy market in 1966, producing the KM range

The new Bedford KM 14 -22 ton trucks being built at Dunstable in October 1966. Expansion projects due for completion by December 1967 would increase truck capacity by 30 per cent. (Vauxhall Motors)

for up to 24 tons gross weight. KM tractor units were up rated from 22 tons after being fitted with a new air actuator on the parking brake. Tate & Lyle were among the well-known liveries using the new range, distributing products from their large sugar refineries. They bought eight 109in wheelbase tractor units in 1967, bringing the total number of Bedfords in their fleet to 143. This was the year when Wilson's Labour government was hoping that something would turn up, in the shape of a successful application to join the common market. Anglo-French agreement seemed more likely, with the first public showing of Concorde in that year. It was also the last year of mainline steam trains and more line closures.

As usual the country was having an economic crisis, credit squeeze and export drive, regardless or perhaps because of all the 'swinging' it was doing. Too many drug and mini skirts and too much rock music, no doubt. Never mind, Bedford joined in the famous 'I'm backing Britain' campaign, exporting 40,000 Bedfords in 1967, earning £31,000,000. Since 1955, 770,000 Bedfords were exported, earning over £407 million. These were the years of the 'brain drain' as brighter folk fed up with Britain's 'stop go' economic policies, fled abroad to where their talents were more valued and less taxed. For those who wanted to get away a little less permanently there was always the Bedford Dormobile, sales being encouraged by the slogan: 'When you buy a Dormobile you buy a country cottage, and a place by the sea, and a mountain hideaway all at the same time.' Readers were advised to try camping, with the slogan 'buy now, pay later.' Curiously, Belfast was described by *Vauxhall Motorist* as 'a motorist's paradise' – when the sectarian troubles there were about to re-ignite.

A KM from the 1960s still hard at work on the island of Jersey in May 2001. (Robert Cook)

At least haulage opportunities looked good, not surprisingly considering the demise of railways and efforts to catch up with the housing shortage. Tippers were ever popular along with de-mountable bodies. The latter could save operators £60-70 per vehicle because operators were taxed on unloaded weight. The Dunstable plant was, accordingly, busy producing 360 Bedfords, including, CKDs, vans and PSVs, a day and with a £6.75 million expansion plan underway. For want of space, the parts centre moved to Toddington, releasing 476,000sq.ft of space, increasing the truck area to 2,231,117sq.ft.

New plating regulations came into force in January 1968. The carriers licensing system was phased out, meaning that 1 million vehicles under 30cwt would not need a goods licence and half a million A, B and C licences would be abolished. The distinction between hire and reward and own account operation would disappear to be replaced by an operators' licensing system. A special authorised quality control authorisation would oversee journeys exceeding 100 miles. This new regulation from Wilson's Labour government would affect 70,000 heavier vehicles over five tons and driving time would be limited to nine hours driving in an eleven hour day and sixty hour week. The tachograph was born and enforceable following legislation the following July. Haulage entered the modern and motorway age.

Car developments also proceeded apace, behind the scenes development always well ahead of the latest road models. Streamlining became more important on new motorways, as power and speed increased. At the time, Vauxhall calculated that a 25 per cent increase in power gave only a 10–12 per cent increase in speed due to increasing drag and rolling resistance. Below 37mph rolling resistance was much greater than drag. Beyond this speed, air (drag) increases faster so that

79 per cent of power is necessary to push the car through the air and only 21 per cent to overcome rolling resistance. Hence it became crucial to study aerodynamic shape. J.E. Gudgin, AMI Mech.Eng, one of Vauxhall's experimental engineers wrote, in 1965:

> 'The ideal aerodynamic shape can be seen in supersonic aircraft or even high speed jet liners, but the body shape of a motor car must be a compromise, since a perfectly streamlined car is not only impossible, but is also unacceptable in terms of price and function. It would also be difficult to reconcile aerodynamic shape with the kind of appearance the stylist finds acceptable to the customers.'

Among other significant innovations, radial tyres were being advertised as a 'flatter sort of tyre and the Viva was getting revved up for a sporting career. Alternators began to replace dynamos, overcoming the problem of putting out high power at lower engine speeds without offering too much at high speed, becoming optional on Vivas and Crestas in 1967, and standard on the Viscount sixes. The Viva SL was announced early in 1967, along with the Viva SL, with the option of the Borg Warner Model 35 automatic gearbox, combining a three speed planetary gear train with a three element torque converter, for more smoothness, flexibility and economy. At speeds below 40mph, second gear could be selected simply by pressing the accelerator. The planetary gear set, within a larger gear, provided the higher range of gears, the idea being to offer an infinite ratio, like an electric motor. The torque convertor was designed to make a fluid coupling between the engine and rear axle, as with the hydra matic box. The coupling flings oil from a driven set of vanes into a passive set of vanes. It is effectively a clutch and can only deliver the amount of torque supplied. Extra torque is provided when the engine throttles away and decreases once the driven vanes have gained momentum. The torque converter is almost a complete automatic system, but needs assistance from planetary gears. There is no need to shift these gears manually. For the low gear range, the sun gear unlocks the planet gears so that they roll around the internal gear, effectively driving a set of teeth inside the large wheel containing them, and so providing high torque from this cluster of smaller gears. The system was new to Britain in 1965, but was already a best selling option on 13 million GM cars in the US.

Six-cylinder models for 1966 were announced at the end of 1965, earning these comments from the *Daily Express*: 'The most elegant cars Vauxhalls have ever produced. The Cresta de Luxe, 15ft 7in of superb good looks.' Features included twin headlamps of the new sealed beam variety, bright wheel trim, rectangular fog lights, a 3.3 litre 123bhp OHV engine with a four-speed floor gear shift optional . Knee-bashing doors were lost in Vauxhall's past, and so Mary Collins of the *Daily Express* could proclaim: 'And praise be it is possible for a woman to get into a Cresta gracefully.'

The new six-cylinder car had a larger fuel tank, up from 10.8 gals to 15, the wheelbase was unchanged at 107.5in, overall height was 55.6in, and luggage

Of course, London was the place to be for the young and glamorous and that definition had to include this 1964 Victor 101 and its occupants. (Vauxhall Motors)

capacity 15.28cu.ft. A space curving approach to panels followed the Victor 101's success. Pronounced vertical curvature of doors and windows allowed the vehicle to be half an inch narrower than the previous model, helping toward a 44 per cent gain in rigidity, improving quietness of ride and handling. The variable rate rear suspension stiffened progressively under increasing load or road conditions by adding a helper leaf below the main leaves of the spring. An estate version remained available until 1968.

The very technical complexity of cars could intimidate women. However, in June 1967 a lady wrote to *Vauxhall Motorist*, thanking them for publishing articles on road safety, adding:

> '...for although I read your magazine regularly, I sometimes feel I am trespassing... There are few people more likely to not have that self righteous attitude to driving than a perceptive member of the weaker sex... that woman driver image is believed in by the majority of people and resentment of it gradually matures into a determination to be a better driver.'

What might be judged better driving depends on what sort of driver a person wants to be. Women have fewer accidents going from A to B, but still lack in the grand prix department, while many men like to use public roads for racing driver fantasies. However, it is arguable that without the male penchant for risk taking there would be no mechanised transport in the first place. The Jack Brabhams of this world have played a vital role in bringing us ever better and safer cars by exploring the limits of known technology while searching for something better. Thus in 1967 Jack Brabham Conversions Ltd set about the task of Brabhamising the Vauxhall Viva for the race track. Jack told Vauxhall Motorist in April 1967:

> 'What we set out to produce was an inherently safe car with just that extra pop for snappier acceleration and even safer overtaking, but without the sacrifice of fuel economy. We have succeeded simply by modifying Vauxhall's already lively '90' engine and exhaust system, as we found outstanding road holding and handling qualities of the latest Viva more than adequate without modification.'

The Brabham organisation added twin CD Stromberg carburettors, new inlet manifold, high duty main bearing, separate 'pancake' air cleaners for the 1,159cc high compression (90:1) engine and a Brabham big bore straight through exhaust with single silencer and chromed tail pipe.

Cars drivers were enjoying quicker journey times, but motorway traffic was increasing rapidly. Trucks were becoming a nuisance, looking like a snails grand prix as they struggled to overtake three abreast, or even just blocked all lanes for the fun of it. The solution came in the summer of 1967 when trucks were banned from the third lane. The Road Safety Act of that year also established drink driving tests and more Vauxhall Viva Panda cars went on the beat to stop the miscreants getting away.

Product development saw the release of new FD Victors in 1967. Basil Cardew, of the *Daily Express*, described them as outstandingly attractive. The Victor and Victor 2000 had the same type engine in different power versions, 1,599cc (83 bhp) and 1,975cc (104bhp) with a big toothed and flexible belt made of

This image of the of the HB Viva's large door opening, reveals that design had advanced a long way beyond Frank Ford's knee bashers. The rather personable driver also demonstrates the correct way to exit the vehicle in an age of rising hemlines. (Vauxhall Motors)

neoprene, with glass-fibre tension members driving the overhead camshaft . The style was slightly inflated Viva and presaging the rival MKIII Ford Cortina. The engine was smooth running, belt silent and complex tappet adjustment was eliminated by a patent system of hexagonal keys. Large valves and hemispherical combustion chambers added to performance. The exhaust was four branch, suspension new, the 2000 had an alternator and pre-engaged starter, while the smaller engine used a generator and inertia type starter. A standard three-speed column change was fitted unless the four-speed floor option, with Laycock overdrive was chosen. The two litre also had the option of Borg Warner automatic gearbox and low profile 6.2X13 tyres. Prices were £819 for the Victor and £910 for the Victor 2000.

Vauxhall Motors had begun life showing an enthusiasm for class and speed. En route to the swinging sixties it had moved toward the sedate and country estate. By the end of the 1960s it had regained some of the sporty image, while not deserting its more stalwart customers. One such was Mrs Bate, featured by *Vauxhall Motorist* in February 1969. She began driving Vauxhalls in 1914. The report conjured up a wonderful image:

'To step into Mrs Bate's delightful home in Regency Cheltenham is to step back to an age of elegance and quality that is rare these days...

Pete Condon holds up the recalcitrant 'roo bar', which was supposed to never come off, on the cross-country jouney to Perth. (Pete Condon)

'Mrs Bate ...looking more like 50... bubbles with vitality...

'She is a favourite and much-liked customer with all the staff at Haines & Stamp, the Vauxhall main dealers in Cheltenham from whom she has been buying cars for years...

'In fifty-five years of driving Mrs Bate has experienced many incidents. There was the morning she was driving from London to Brighton for breakfast many years ago. Near Redhill she collected a puncture and while pondering the problem a pleasant man came up offering help. With brisk efficiency he jacked up the car and changed the wheel. It was not until he'd finished that Mrs Bate discovered the man was an inmate of a nearby lunatic asylum.'

Satisfied customers came from far and wide, many cherishing memories of past and much-loved models. Australian Pete Condon recalled the February 1970 when he and his mate Trevor decided to go to Perth for a working holiday for six months. Pete said:

'Trevor owned a 1963 Vauxhall Cresta and me a 1967 Holden. I sold my car as we only needed one for the journey and Trevor's was a much better, more comfortable and well equipped than an Aussie car. It was automatic, with heater and carpets. First we set off to Tullamarine Airport where our mate was working as a plumber. He had a bull bar which he had made for us and welds it on to the front saying: 'It will NEVER come off!' This was important because we were going into kangaroo country and didn't want to wipe out the

Arrival in Western Australia and Pete looks relieved, though the 1963 Cresta had performed well and was much more comfortable than native GMC Holdens. (Pete Condon)

Trevor and his trusty Vauxhall Cresta on arrival in Perth. (Vauxhall Motors)

car by hitting a kangaroo. We drove on to Perth, across three states, through Adelaide and on to Ceduna and the start of the Nullabor Plain, which is all unmade road for about 300km. We had to drive on the wrong side of the road because of all the pot holes, but it was OK because there was nothing else on the road. We were hiking along when BANG. The car hits a huge rock in the road, goes up and over it and rips the bull bar half off one side. It's hanging there so we had to stop. Trevor was cursing the bull bar which was welded on and would never come off. We jump on it, hit with crowbars, but it does finally come off and we leave it up against the side of a tree and drive off. We drove to Perth and drove around in this car for six months and never had a moment of trouble with it. Then we went home. On the way back, on the same route, we were hiking along, coming up to a tight bend when the exhaust falls off. Trevor slows down a lot to take the curve, the steering spanned right and the car went left. A bolt in the linkage had come off. Luckily for us the exhaust had come off first so we'd already slowed for the bend. Other than that the car never let us down, and we got home in one piece.'

Pete was so impressed that on his return when he passed a car yard with a green Vauxhall Cresta out the front for sale at $400, he went in and bought it. He said: 'It was a great car. Vauxhalls were so much better than any of the other cars that were around at the time, because of all the extras that were included as standard.' There were many good reasons for being prejudiced towards buying a Vauxhall, it was agreed across the world.

CHAPTER TEN

EXTRAORDINARY
LATITUDE

Cars were getting faster, safer and more reliable. The age of vinyl roof options had arrived, in black or parchment, costing £8 10s for Victors and £8 for Vivas – advertisements said vinyl added distinction. The popularity of motoring was ever ascendant, with AA membership reaching 4 million in 1969 – only six years after it had hit 3 million. Car development for an ever more discriminate and demanding public required the most intensive testing and no more of Frank Ford's belting down the straightest roads that he could find. Public roads were too crowded and test speeds far too high for that sort of thing. Thus, stage one of a £3.5 million project to build a test course at Millbrook was complete. It involved excavating 2 million cubic yards of earth, with speed banking created and neutral steer speeds in lanes of 40, 50, 60, 75 and 100mph safely – and 125mph in the outside lane. There were hill test routes, with varying slopes and curves over a 3.25mph circuit, as well as a rugged cross-country route for trucks, with muddy areas and king-sized pot holes – during the war army trucks had been tested in the ponds at Luton's Wardown Park. Stage Two was completed by early 1971, comprising a tough rough track with concrete blocks, one to two inches proud, scattered at random. 24,000 trees were also planted on site.

The first Bedford trucks were made in 1931 and in spite of having no test track, there were miles of open country to test and build the toughest trucks of the day. By March 1969 production reached 1.5 million, with former aristocrat turned Technology Minister Anthony Wedgewood Benn being chosen to drive number 1.5 million off the production line. The vehicle was a left-hand drive 16-tonner. Like 49 per cent of all Bedords ever built, it went for export. Bedford also announced their new CF range and KMS tipper in November 1969. The CF 35 cwt had a 126in wheelbase, twin rear wheels, hinged and de luxe cab options with hinged or sliding doors. There were five basic models and body variants. The new type marked the end of the remarkable CA which had been in production since 1952, with 370,445 units made. Another famous model, the four-wheel drive R type, ceased production in 1970, being replaced by the MK.

Part of the WH Smith's fleet of Bedford CF vans when at a time when the company were untroubled by huge trading losses and they were still close to their newspaper sales roots. Struggling in 2004, to meet competitions from supermarkets and other chains, the group announced £100 million losses. (Vauxhall Motors)

Speed restrictions had eased up on trucks and piece work caused some drivers to race. Racing, however, belongs on the track and the purpose of works racing teams has been to improve the product whilst enabling drivers and race crowds to enjoy the spectacle. By 1969 aeronautical engineer Bill Bydenstein had emerged as Vauxhall's race tuner extraordinary. He designed a camshaft allowing, in his words:

> 'oodles of oomph' from about 300rpm up to nearly 8,000. Tecalamit fuel injection replaced the big Weber carburettors, allowing 200hp to find its way to the clutch. The noise that gets to the atmosphere via the curly exhaust manifold is exhilarating to say the least.'

The Blydenstein name became synonymous with Vauxhall racing in the 1970s, with much spin off for production models. Bill developed the Weber carburettor and air cleaner for Vauxhall 1,600cc engines. He drove his last race in the 1,258cc Viva Special at Lydden Hill, afterwards devoting himself to improving standard car handling and efficiency. His achievements were exemplified in the latest Viva and Firenza ranges. The latter began life as an attractive but under powered (63hp) sporty Viva, reaching its apogee in the 1975 coupe. This car had a lowered floor pan, light alloy wheels and glass fibre nosecap with recessed quad lamps. Capable of 120mph, details included 131 on twin Strombergs, 9.2 compression, and a five-

Gerry Marshall, the team and cars in the early 1970s.

speed ZF gear box. It was an obvious rival to Ford's Capri. A *Vauxhall Motorist* reader, Phillip Green, informed the magazine in June/July 1972:

> 'As a motoring enthusiast I was very sceptical of the Firenza when it was first brought out. I thought it to be very much over-styled and Americanised. I found the exaggerated fast back objectionable. I thought its competitors in the sporty family car range was far better. Since then my father has bought a Firenza 1600 and I have been completely converted. I've found its interior to be pleasant and comfortable, there is ample leg room in the back and the boot is positively huge; just two points where the Firenza comes out on top. The performance and versatility of the engine has grown on me until all other car styling seems outdated. The Firenza is certainly a winner, though it may take a year or so for the rest of the conservative British public to become as convinced as myself.'

The Thames TV Firenza delivered 120mph at 6,000rpm, winning eight out of nine races in 1972. Gerry Marshall soon emerged to show his talent in the Forward Trust Championship races, making a name for himself at Thruxton and Silverstone. Dealer Team Vauxhall was formed to consolidate sporting ventures, and helping investment and prospering in the 2.5 litre engine category. In 1972, Bill Blydenstein informed *Vauxhall Motorist* readers:

Gerry Marshall's Firenza, preserved at the Vauxhall Heritage Centre, Osborne Road, Luton. (Vauxhall Motors)

'Our trusty Thames Televison Firenza in Marshall's capable hands last year scored fourteen outright victories, two seconds, one third place and one retirement... Both engines gave well over 190bhp and over 180lb/ft torque. That Marshall seems able to beat cars with engines of 250 and even 300bhp is perhaps an indication that our horses are strong ones which do not tire easily...'

Bill Blydenstein continued his commentary in that year:

'The results of the RAC rally have just come in as I write. We were all very disappointed when Will Sparrow in the Martin sponsored Group 2 Firenza had to retire when his shock absorbers gave out and his service crew were unable to reach him with repalcement units. In the end the terrific pounding threw the occupants around to such an extent that Will's seat tore lose from its mountings. You cannot drive a rally car hanging on to the steering wheel.'

The Viva GT was also upgraded, receiving a new exhaust with dual front pipes and aluminised silencer, redesigned clutch and throttle cables, distinctive wide Rostyle wheels, and 165/70HR X13 low profile radial tyres as standard. The Victor gained more power from its 108bhp 2000 engine, the SL model having new trim and colour choices. The Ventora II benefited from a revised rear axle ratio of 3.09:I, a 9in clutch, revised gear ratios and an even quieter cruising speed. Seatbelts were fitted, as part of the 'clunk click every trip' culture being promoted

Rows of HB Vivas await export at Liverpool docks in the late 1960s. (Vauxhall Motors)

by DJ Jimmy Saville – a man whose voluntary hospital work put him in regular contact with the consequences of untethered travellers being catapulted from crashing cars.

The Government had founded its own road and vehicle research facilities in Berkshire, but companies like Vauxhall had need of their own. Their 700-acre Millbrook proving ground was very busy in the early 1970s and safety testing was conducted in an impact simulator, using eleven adult dummies, a three year old, six year old and pregnant woman. Millbrook also conducted salt water tests on the Victor Estate car in efforts to combat corrosion. For all of these fine efforts, there was an enduring tendency to treat cars like toys or little personal statements on wheels, embellished by some dubious extras. In this context a *Vauxhall Motorist* reader of March 1972 noted the fashion for nodding dogs etc. on the car's back shelf and had even spotted a Viva with matching toilet roll. Another slightly frenzied reader commented, presumably on the grounds that you can't get too much of a good thing and Beeching had not done enough:

'I have measured many double track railways and have found that they would easily accommodate a 24ft-wide trunk road (even the tunnels are 26½-28ft wide.'

This viewpoint was adumbrated by the first Lord Montague in 1913 when he fantasised about a world of rail tracks ripped up to accommodate cars rattling

There is still a hint of flower power, hinting at the freedoms of the age, in this view of the Magnum 2300 which evolved from the Viva concept, as did the Firenza. There was also an 1800 version. (Vauxhall Motors)

along at 50mph. Television had become a major source of motor advertising and the clamour for more roads on the cheap left little sympathy for rail enthusiasts. Shaw Taylor sparked a trend for TV motoring programmes with his late night show called *Drive* in 1964. This was followed by BBC's *Wheelbase* in the same year. ITV responded with a new show called *Drive in* in 1971. Motoring was

The early 1970s were the heydays of flared trousers and questionable fashion sense, mainly because a lot of youngsters opted for unisex styles. This we can see from the dancers in front of the new Victor FE production line at Luton. Sadly for the men on the line, this was only a promotion for the new model – but this was surely just as well for Vauxhall, as all that glamour could have been distracting, thus harming the company's outstanding reputation. (Vauxhall Motors)

now a complete way of life. Cars were cool and people were flying through their driving tests. A former examiner told the author that if they did not pass 55 per cent of candidates the chief examiner wanted to know why. Norman Sullivan was featured in *Vauxhall Bedford News*, suggesting that test standards were too low in 1969. Meanwhile railway defenders were not giving up without a fight and *Vauxhall Motorist* was keen to be even handed when they published A. Tuck's comments as follows:

'Your correspondent A.I. Walkinson writes with all the unconscious thoughtlessness we have come to expect from those who find it necessary to assert their virility at the steering wheel. He suggests that the railways be turned into motorways. I trust that he will accept

Cars and trains could work together, as this publicity image for the FE Victor denotes, with a 'to die for' girlfriend or wife having apparently delivered her husband to the station, and now he is going to trust her to drive her home without scratching it! Of course, the picture could be open to slightly naughtier interpretations at a time when 'Confessions of...' films were popular on the Big Screen! (Vauxhall Motors)

that the London-Leeds line will be exempted, there being already a parallel motorway, albeit at State expense. I propose to ignore the rather vague political clap trap and concentrate on his unspeakable suggestion and on its effects. What it would do would be to divide the nation into two groups, a privileged group, able to travel, and an unprivileged group, fixed in their homes. The dividing line would be of course, money. In short, the poor would lose the right to travel... Since the war car designers, manufacturers and agents have done an unbelievable job in bringing personal mobility to millions to whom it was formerly unknown; but there remain many people to whom it is not at present possible to extend the benefits of car ownership. To these people the railways are essential ad we have no right to take them away just to make life easier and travel faster for ourselves... The motorist has extraordinary latitude which he should not seek greedily to extend lest he should lose even that which he hath.'

With the price of the Victor de luxe at a reasonable £1,227 in 1972, there undoubtedly were still many British who couldn't afford a car, so there was still life in public service vehicles. In this respect, Bedford had broken new ground with the early 1960s VAL chassis – pre war six wheelers having the second axle at the rear and non steering. The twin steer VAL found fame in the cult film *The Italian Job*. Several different bodies, including horse boxes, a mobile blood collection unit for Zambia and an outside broadcast unit for Southern TV, were built. Designed as a touring coach, early VALs were mainly bodied by Duple and

A preserved VAL offers vintage coach rides at the Bedford gathering in Cambridge, August 2003. (Robert Cook)

Plaxton, but Weyman, Willowbrook and Harrington also supplied bodies for the home market. The 36ft length allowed for seating of between forty-nine and fifty-two people. Bass Hill Coaches in Sydney were among overseas operators to use the VAL. As the coach and bus market narrowed, there was an inevitable amalgamation in the body building world and the famous Duple marque became subsumed within Plaxton's. Meanwhile Dormobile Ltd had become the name for the coachbuilding division of the Martin Walter Group in March 1969.

With so many road accidents involving HGVs it was decided to bring in specific licence categories and testing. Those with six months aggregate driving experience in their class during the twelve months prior to February 1970 were exempt. Road safety was becoming an ever more pressing concern, with serious accidents rising in spite of developments making vehicles much safer. The move toward car-like comfort for truckers encouraged the piecework mentality. Trucking was becoming something of a rat race, with the industry beginning to favour a cowboy culture taken from TV and a world away from Britain's thronging thoroughfares.

Driving is a rather peculiar activity. A lot of folk will say that they play golf but are not very good at it. The same is not true, especially with men, when it comes to driving. More speed and accidents tended to display what cars were made of. Ripped apart on the roadside, they offer food for thought and are not a pretty sight. Particularly to those who never doubt their driving skills, it is the car's fault. Too many drivers saw themselves free spirits, so much so that G. Woodville of Aylesbury informed *Vauxhall Motorist* in February 1973:

As this late 1960s mid-engined SRV Vauxhall concept design work suggests, cars were being designed to go faster all the time, in spite of the 70mph speed limit - temporarily reduced to 50mph in 1974/5 during the fuel crisis. Seat belts were seen as a major safety initiative. (Vauxhall Motors)

'I would certainly support any campaign to encourage people to use seat belts... but I think it would be unenforceable. A better way would be an interlock with the ignition system coupled with the inertia reel type belt which would overcome most objections...

In February 1972, O.H. Brown of Selby, Yorks, informed *Vauxhall Motorist* thus:

'Who'd buy 'em Sir. They don't make cars the way they used to is an oft heard cry, implying that today's standards of workmanship and design are inferior to those of bygone days. I am not qualified to express an opinion on the truth or otherwise of thjis. However, I do know that twenty years ago the sight of a motorist struggling with a broken-down vehicle was fairly common, whereas now seeing a driver in trouble is comparitively rare. This is with a much car population.'

The UK car market increased by 18 per cent over the first eleven months of 1971, with Vauxhall registrations rising by 29 per cent. Bedford van sales, no doubt a response to the new CF range, rose by 39 per cent.

Vauxhall-Bedford sales rose 20 per cent worldwide, totalling 324,186 vehicles. Car sales rose 37½ per cent to 143,837 and Bedford truck and van sales went up by 19½ per cent to 63,901 – a new record despite a shrinking world market. Over

Design team workers putting the final touches to a clay model in the styling studio in the late 1970s. Aerodynamics were increasingly important to road holding and fuel economy. (Vauxhall Motors)

70 per cent of Bedfords were exported. Product development proceeded apace as the industry moved into the computer age. Engineer Frank Ford moved into product information. He recalled:

'The library was under my control, with seven people working for me. The job was to produce product specification, a document giving technical information about the cars and trucks. At that time we had to have different standards and features for different countries. The FA Victor had even been renamed the Envoy for export. When we did our product specification we had to provide various appendices accordingly. I said we should contact our representatives in each country to find out what they needed for type approval. I made this multi-page document, everything having to be in metric and Imperial measure. Having got the format almost sorted, I had to go to Vienna when the Vectra and Viva GT were being introduced to Austria. General Motors Austria gave a day to motoring pressmen, organised by SMMT and I had to be Mr Vauxhall for the day. It was a fascinating experience with a banquet in the evening. The Austrian police closed a three mile section of road for the day, providing a circuit around a hunting lodge. It was an event for all British cars. An unauthorised Austrian stuck an E Type Jaguar down a culvert and the press had all day to try them out. During the day I was chauffeured into Vienna to talk to GM men about type approval and new specifications. I produced quite a thick document so that we could send the same one everywhere.'

In line with the new global approach, the company unveiled their Victor Transcontinental in 1972. The *Financial Times* spoke favourably: 'It will appeal to those who value an inexpensive high performance car with plenty of passenger and luggage space.' *Sporting Life* reported that the model 'certainly represented good value for money'. *Motor* considered that the 2300SL felt lively enough and pulled 100mph in overdrive top without much run up, so there shouldn't be many complaints about performance'. The *Daily Telegraph* reported in the same vein: '...even with the driver's seat adjusted well back there's room for three tall passengers in the rear seat.' The Ventora offered an even higher specification, with 3.3 litre, six-cylinder engine and 140bhp. Such luxury, complete with seven-dial instrument panel in walnut fascia was luxury at £1,768.

Motoring writer Harry Hassent bought his first Vauxhall from Kingston Hill Motors in June 1972, it was registration OMT 677K. His impressions were recorded in the October/November *Vauxhall Motorist*:

'For years my personal transport had been sporty little cars, all exhaust noise and hard suspension...A respectable family saloon decked out with leather bound steering wheel, that's what I thought of the VX 4/90. Within the first 3,000 miles it began to filter through to me that I was wrong...

Sunday lunchtime- arrived at St Clair 3,855 miles on the clock...

The reverse ruin went just as smoothly...

Though Vauxhall don't stick on the fiddling GT labels, the VX 4/90 is the 1970s version of the true Gran Tourismo. It has long legs – you can if you wish, roll happily through the countryside in overdrive speeds up to the ton... and still have something left... Between 50 and 70 the car has real push against the seat acceleration – plenty of power to pass in top with complete safety; drop into third or overdrive third and you can get the full benefit of that 2,279cc engine...'

Such capability, though meaningful on the Continent was somewhat hamstrung at home. Transport was, like most other matters in Britain, in crisis. Leslie Huckfield was the Labour Transport Minister in waiting. A former lorry driver, he kept his hand in during the holidays, managing to get a picture of himself outside Parliament, with a Bedford TK, in the *Daily Mirror* and to be featured in *Vauxhall Motorist* in 1972. Son of an engine driver and product of two universities, he was the youngest MP at twenty-four, telling the magazine:

'...generally speaking, my party believes in molly coddling the railways and messing up the economics of road haulage. The Tory Party, on the other hand is too pro road... I believe we have to make the maximum use of all forms of transport... The driving test is in serious need of revision; MoT test are a load of rubbish and the breathalyser just isn't working... We've got to accept pretty stringent controls. And for my part I'd rather see a crack-down on parking than say an annual charge for bringing a car in,,, the toll idea would be difficult to administer.'

Pollution was a growing concern, but noting would hold motor traffic growth. Driving was the ultimate freedom. Since early days, lead was the key ingredient to smooth engine running, absorbing the shock of each cylinder explosion. An alternative was needed since it was particularly poisonous to the young and a large constituent of city air. Thus, in 1972, the Environment Secretary announced the phased reduction of lead in petrol by nearly a half over three years, from 0.64 grams per litre to 0.55 at the end of 1973 and 0.45 by the end of 1975. In the same year the Government announced that the London-Oxford M40 would be extended to Birmingham.

While motorways should have made driving safer, they were being treated by many men as race tracks. Thus the term 'motorway madness' was born and foggy days became synonymous with carnage. It seemed too many thought they were race drivers, though clearly lacking the natural talent of Vauxhall's Gerry Marshall.

There were other hazards on the motorway as Egon Ronay pointed out through the pages of the June/July 1973 edition of *Vauxhall Motorist*:

'If Little Chef (a Trust Houses Forte Subsidiary): 'If Little Chef ever lay their table along the motorways they'll run most of the established M Way eating places out of business... The two most appalling things about these motorway cafeterias is the squalor and their service. I've stopped 10 minutes waiting for a coffee. When I take it to a table I'm faced with dirty crocks, overflowing ashtrays and enough waste food to feed a shed full of swine.'

CHAPTER ELEVEN

MORE TO WORRY ABOUT

Britain had more to worry about than grotty motorway services in the early 1970s, but those stations were undoubtedly symbolic of a general malaise. The national economic growth rate declined from 2.5 per cent in 1969 to 2 per cent in 1970 and 1.7 per cent in 1971. Heath's Tory government saw a solution through membership of the Economic Community while the National Union of Coal Miners saw the solution in the removal of Heath. Not surprisingly this was not a good time for selling large cars. L.S. Patterson informed readers of *Vauxhall Motorist* in June 1973 that he had owned ten Crestas from 1955 to 1972 and regretted the demise of the name. He wrote:

> 'Strange that this fine car never achieved the volume of sales it deserved. Neither did its only close competitor. British motorists are terrified by the thought of buying and running a big car with a big engine. They imagine the running costs will be high but this is not the case. A big engine, big by British standards, that rarely needs any attention. I have been told that the 3.3 litre Vauxhall engine turns in happily 75,000 or 100,000 miles without ever needing the head lifted. Oil consumption is almost nil... Petrol consumption is better than on most cars of smaller capacity – 25mpg on anything but all town motoring. Many a 1,500cc engine cannot truthfully equal that figure... overall, if ever there was a trouble free car, the Cresta was one. And now it has gone, and it will be difficult to find a replacement...'

The world moves on but big engines were certainly not defunct, though safety was becoming more important than size. Cars were going faster regardless of cars and Transport Minister John Peyton was considering an 80mph speed limit. Thus it was comforting when Dunlop announced the 'total mobility tyre.' Following a puncture, the tyre partially reflated so that motorists could continue their journey at 50mph for another 100 miles. To the same end, drivers could purchase the Avon Safety tyre which was designed to keep a blown tyre on the rim. Sadly, however safe Vauxhall made their cars, every one would be a lethal weapon in the wrong hands and there have never been enough policemen to keep bad drivers in order. Police class one driver Bill Clarke from Yorks and North East Constabulary told *Vauxhall News* in May 1973: 'We go into bends slow and come out fast. They go into bends fast and don't come out.'

Bill's force had just received twenty-six Vauxhall Victor estate cars and he was one of 187 men commanded by Chief Superintendent Ted Field. Ted was responsible for 2.5 million acres. The response time in this large area was thirteen-fifteen minutes. Bill said :

'We need a big engine which runs in a lazy fashion. We want to get high mileage's without the everlasting need for tuning to keep them on top form. Only last year we had a fighter crash... searched for a fortnight before we found the lad buried in a snow drift wrapped in his parachute...'

Police training was not the only route to skilled driving with some outstanding driving schools working to inculcate students with survival skills on increasingly crowded carriageways. Denise McCann took over the chairmanship of BSM in 1957 and by 1973, during which time 2 million trained with her instructors, Vauxhall counted her as an influential and valued customer. This was not surprising considering BSM operated 1,200 cars dispersed through 160 branch offices. Although Vauxhalls found favour in the firm's fleet, this diminutive and well-dressed lady counted Ferraris, Aston Martins. Porsches and a personal Rolls-Royce Corniche among her favourite forms of transport.

Miss McCann became assistant MD in 1951 and chairman when founder S.C.H. Roberts died. Founded in 1910, before driving tests, by 1973 the school was teaching over 200,000 a year, covering 40 million miles yearly and generating income of £5 million. She ran a tight organisation, one employee commenting:

'Several people, some of our area managers, are extremely frightened of her. When people do stupid things she can get very sharp indeed... People come out of her room looking very flushed, I can tell you'

On the subject of women drivers, Miss McCann told *Vauxhall Motorist* that women were more apprehensive and cautious but less likely to be involved in serious accidents. She told *Vauxhall Motorist*:

'A good driver is a good driver regardless of sex. You can always spot him- or her- because he will exhibit what I call the four Cs: Courtesy, Consideration, Care and Concentration.'

On working women, one of her male colleagues said:

'Quite honestly I never think about it. I used to wonder what it might be like working for a woman and I don't think I could work for any other woman I have met in business. But here, well, we're totally unconscious of the fact that we work for one.'

Meanwhile *Vauxhall Motorist* carried a feature on women at work, under the heading 'Thank Heavens for Little Girls' and showing some rather glamorous young ladies, such as 'Linda Jean Gill, 19' who 'operates a machine that finishes tappets for OHC (Overhead Camshaft) engines'. Linda Jean was described with mild superlatives that would incite legal action today, to the effects that she added glamour to the work place and 'would not be a stay at home wife.'

Of particular benefit to women, technological improvements steadily reduced the physical demands of driving but were not to everyone's liking. A letter from D.H. Machlachlan, of Galashiels, to the August–September 1973 edition of *Vauxhall Motorist* commented:

> 'A plague on your automatic chokes. I have a 1972 Viva SL. Starting from cold its minimum speed was 15mph. To brake at a halt sign or a right angle bend meant an almost certain skid on slippery roads. I had some narrow escapes, and for the first time in twenty-six years of carefree motoring I became frightened to use the car if road conditions were bad. I have had a manual choke fitted, though I did grudge paying for it. Why not give the buyer a choice of an automatic or manual choke.'

Old habits were dying hard for some but with Bill Blydenstein and Gerry Marshall pushing the company name with regular competition success and advancing race performance, along with factory experts, Vauxhall were not going to get stuck in the mud. Existing electrical ignitions were simply a high ratio coil switched by high voltage transistors with a contact breaker interrupting the transistor's base current. Ignition systems had lagged behind engine improvements. A new electronic ignition kit was being sold by AMC Electronics, offering improvements. Working against the base line of a four-cylinder engine needing two sparks per revolution at 6,000rpm and a six-cylinder needing three sparks per revolution, the kit was able to offer virtually constant voltage output over the whole speed range to over 10,000rpm for a four-cylinder and 7,000rpm for a six-cylinder. The new idea involved a capacitor discharge system, using a transistor inverter to charge up a capacitor to about 400 Volts. The capacitor stores the energy and when the contact breaker opens, a silicon-controlled rectifier is triggered and discharges the capacitor through the coil.

Better electronics supported further engine developments and fuel economy. Frank Costin designed the Ventora V8 which was built at Bill Byldenstein's Shepreth works. Based on the standard FE Ventora bodyshell with fibreglass doors, rear wings, boot lid, front nose section and air dam, it weighed 21cwt. Engine and driver Gerry Marshall sat further back to give 50/50 weight distribution. Frank designed the suspension, allowing for a five litre Holden Repco racing unit, based on General Motors racing unit, producing 500bhp at 7,600rpm and 392ilb/ft torque. The engine was used to power some of the Holden range and was developed with the most successful Formula 5000 racing in Australia, by Repco and Lucas fuel injection. A dry sump was built into the rear of the car, along with two eight-gallon fuel tanks. The gearbox was a Warner Super unit with Hurst shift and the car made its debut at Silverstone on 6 October 1973 followed by Brands Hatch All Stars the next day and then on to the London Motor Show.

The year 1973 had been good for Vauxhall racing, with Bill Bydenstein observing that it was most encouraging to see, during the 1973 rally season, so many Vauxhalls being entered in all sorts of rallies, from small to national and international. Many of the competing Vauxhalls were perfectly standard cars with just a few suspension options. He said that the 2.3 litre unit lent itself very well to rallying as it was extremely robust and gives out the sort of immense torque curve that it is appreciated on the tight sections and was more important than all out power.

With 1973 ending in fallout from the miner's strike and a three day week, energy was in short supply the following year and motor sport would suffer along with the rest of the motoring public from increased costs and a 50mph speed limit. Petrol reached 58p a gallon. Still nothing would stop the British buying cars, even if they did have to fight their way to the petrol pumps sometimes. Gerry Marshall, 32, Vauxhall saloon car racer and a very successful motor dealer ploughed on with his career. Weighing seventeen stone, *Vauxhall Motorist* carried a feature in April, including the lines:

> 'In some people's minds there is a connection between his weight (Gerry's) and his wins and they think of him as a heavyweight who pushes the opposition out of the way. This is not Gerry's eye view. 'I am amazed at what people do to me!' He says. 'I am always avoiding other peoples' accidents.'

Interviewed in his busy office: 'There's a lot of psychology' says Gerry, talking about motor racing, but that applies to his business too. Back to racing: 'If you can lean on someone's boot lid and shake your fist it upsets 'em... keeps people on their toes...'

Born in St Neots, the son of a builders' merchant, Gerry attended Harrow High School, before apprenticeship with a high-class ironmongers and locksmiths. He gave it all up to work for a 'Dealer's Delivery, Car Collection and on to partnership with Bill Bydenstein when he was racing Mini 850s. The partnership moved on to modify and race Vauxhalls in the late 1960s. Not surprisingly, he steered the V8 Ventora to victory on its first outing, beating the V8 Strawson (ex Mick Hill) V8 Capri 5 litre. Continually looking for novelty in motor racing, the Blydenstein enterprise even used a modified VX4/90 caravan racing, not something one would like to see encouraged on the public highway!

Not to be outpaced, Vauxhall's sister company kept pace with changing markets, announcing the TM range as part of a £53 million expansion programme. Bedford sales drives had proved effective across Europe, with Holland becoming a good customer. Tony De Uries' affection for the marque started as a boy in the early 1980s. His father drove a municipal vehicle in his home town of Zaanstad, Assendelfi. It was a little TK Bedford and Tony used to help his father clean his truck.

> 'I grew up with the Bedford, it was part of my life. My girlfriend shared my interest and in 1994 I bought my first TM. It was in very bad condition. I bought it because I thought it

A 1981 TM pictured at Aylesbury Fire station in May 1997, where it had the grim job of helping to clear up the mess of rather too many road crashes. (Robert Cook)

A more glamorous job for this TM involves hauling the Marlboro Grand Prix Racing team's equipment in the late 1970s. Life was looking good for Bedford. (Vauxhall Motors)

Bedford enthusiast Tony De Uries on a visit from Holland, pictured at Vauxhall's Osborne Road HQ. He is holding a picture of himself as a boy, in front of two Dutch owned TMs. (Robert Cook)

was the only one left in Holland. There was a dealer in Sandhom who sold the most TMs in Holland. Bedford had previously sold much smaller trucks, this was what their dealer networks were geared up for. The TM engine was high revving. The highest gear on the box was too low, with not enough power. They were the Detroit diesels. Some people thought these engines had been sabotaged by the contractors who built them. I asked a mechanic at Ellesmere about this but he couldn't say. I know they never sold many TMs in Holland. There was a problem with the head gasket. They never did more than 100,000 miles before they blew up. I have heard them called English rubbish. Apart from the TMs, Bedfords were very popular in Holland because you could get two for the price of one Mercedes. But I think they stayed too long with the same model. They were good for short distances in the 1950s and 1960s, but old fashioned by the 1980s.'

At the time, however, TM prospects looked good, developing into a range of forty models from 16-44 gross tonnes and from two-axle rigids for draw bar trailers to the TM 3800 Tractor unit which could operate above the then current 32-ton gross legal limit, and with sleeper cab option. The British Army were among many customers and continuing a long tradition of buying Bedfords.

CHAPTER TWELVE

CHANGING FAST

The second wave of TMs appeared in mid-1975, at the same time petrol hit 73p a gallon and Britain's economic prospects seemed as gloomy as ever, in spite of the prospects of North Sea oil wealth. Vauxhall was looking towards more general use of glassfibre panels to cut weight and improve aerodynamics by curving the perspex of side windows. In mid-1975 came the announcement of the compact Chevette, showcased at the Geneva Motor Show and described by Vauxhall Vice Chairman, Bob Price, as a truly European car. On the Total Economy Drive, over 1,200 hard miles, the car achieved an impressive 47.31mpg. The VX4/90, then retailing for £1,661.83 (an extra £111.58 for automatic), also received pound stretcher treatment from an improved carburettor.

It was International Woman's Year in 1975 and fittingly with the trend, the Tories chose Mrs Thatcher to lead them. Value for money would become the swan song of the 1970s because there is very little evidence that Britain benefited from yet another politician's promises. Manufacturing would take a pounding from Tory intentions to make British industry 'leaner and fitter'. General Motors' British branch would ride the storm, but sadly the treasured and unique *Vauxhall Motorist* made its last edition in October/November of that year.

The tone of that edition was up-beat, looking forward to some futuristic designs and back at past glories. The letters page opened with 'Winner for Britain' and a reader's praise for the Chevette L which reader A. Buchanan had taken delivery of on his seventy-second birthday. He wrote:

'I have owned and driven sixty-two cars, keeping them not more than one year, some less. My last dozen at least have been of foreign make. In the Chevette I'm sure that you have a winner for Vauxhall Motors Britain.'

G. Moss praised his Viva's economy:

'I have just returned from holiday, and kept an accurate record of petrol bought and the amount used. I find it covered 659 miles on 17.1 gallons of petrol, equalling 38.538mpg in my Viva HC (1973 model).'

Once again charming young ladies add the finishing touch to this Chevette promotion. Such an approach would soon be criticised in a fast changing world, and incipient political correctness. So it is nice to look back on a seemingly more innocent world. Vauxhall had to adapt to the changing world, creating stronger links with GMC in Europe. The Chevette marked the change, owing much to Opel mechanics being married to the Viva engine. (Vauxhall Motors)

R. Dawson wrote from Belfast:

'During these times when British cars are being criticised I feel I must thank all concerned for the efficient car I have purchased – a Viva SL. This car was purchased from Moffett of Brougham Street, Belfast. From the first moment I entered their showroom and met their salesman (Mr McCullough) I was treated with respect and individual attention... I have just finished a Continental holiday lasting five weeks (3,000 miles) and from the moment I left my house until my return, the car's performance was of an excellence beyond compare...

Praise continued as T.A. Hunt's words were recorded:

'...until last year, I had never owned a Vauxhall and in the past have had trouble with various makes of British cars. Last October I purchased an 1800 Magnum and have now completed 20,000 trouble-free miles. I use the car at work and drive about 25,000 miles per year. I don't drive slowly, or how a car is supposed to be driven, by the book I mean, and that is the reason I chose a Magnum rather than a Viva...'

From further afield, R.M. Bell wrote from Bundanoon, Australia, under the heading

'Must you go?' I am writing to ...express my regret that the magazine will no longer be available. I enjoyed reading the *Motorist* very much, as it gave me an insight into the Vauxhall industry as well as a great deal of information on technical matters. I feel that all Vauxhall owners, and especially the overseas owners, were kept informed of the advances and also places of interest in the stories in *Motorist* and will be greatly miss the magazine...'

Bill Blydenstein penned his final column for *Vauxhall Motorist* readers, including the lines:

'Looking back over nearly five years of engineering development, it is very interesting to browse through earlier copies of *Vauxhall Motorist*. In 1970 Gerry Marshall and the Shaw and Kilburn Viva GT had already made their mark on the saloon car racing scene, both in club and international racing. Our best result that year was when we took the Group 2 Viva GT to Spa where Gerry finished a close fourth overall... Internationally we scored some resounding successes by picking up the Swedish Ice racing Championships both 1970 and 1971. Des Donnelly ruled the roost in Ireland and Phillip de Freitas and his friends in Guyana and later Brian Ibrahim of Trinidad started dominating the competition scene in the Caribbean.

'The big event of 1971 was the formation of Dealer Team Vauxhall, a logical development when Vauxhall dealers all over the country decided they wanted a part of the limelight. Our biggest victory of 1971 was when Gerry Marshall won the main event of the day at Mondello Park near Dublin. Clever people, the Irish; having studied form they invited David Brodie in the 2.1 litre BDA-engined Escort as well as Mick Hill's all-conquering 5 litre V8 Capri. Their own Alec Poole was a potential winner in the 180bhp turbocharged Mini, potentially the fastest Mini of all time. Our own Gerry, second time out in the 2.6 single- cam Viva GT, also seemed a very good bet on the tight Mondello circuit. So it proved. Gerry Marshall won in the end, the lead changing several times ...1973 saw the advent of the twin cam engine. DTV were able to buy the remaining stock of 904 Lotus engine equipment. These 16-valve cylinder heads had been developed on the 1968/69 Vauxhall cylinder blocks. We were therefore able to build full racing engines to 2.3 litre capacity once we got some 16-valve pistons made, initially by Hepworth and Grandage, later by Cosworth... Last year (1974) really gave us the big breakthrough we had wanted in rallying. Will Sparrow, now driving for DTV, scored a superb string of successes winning the RAC Group 1 outright... Bringing this account up to date, our decision to build all the Ventora V8 bits into a Firenza bodyshell proved to be a shrewd one. Built in just over four months by Gerry Johnstone, Geoff Hall and Dick Waldock with design supervision by Frank Costin, the car has given Gerry Marshall the opportunity to provide some memorable moments. Among his best victories this year were his two wins at Mondello Park and of course his shattering win at Silverstone at the British Grand Prix meeting. The car is by no means fully developed nor is it giving the sort of power which Gerry would like. It is, however a rather unique machine, a worthy successor to the V8 Ventora. ...A fascinating five years. Times are changing fast. The days are over when *Vauxhall Motorist* magazine united all Vauxhall competitors from all over the world and gave

Cowley and Wilson, now part of the Lex Vauxhall group which absorbed Shaw and Kilburn, ran these popular show rooms on the A5 Watling street, near Bletchley, seen here in the early 1980s. (Colin Stacey)

them perhaps some feeling of unity and sense of purpose. It is to be hoped that this sense of achievement will continue even if the magazine is no more.'

G. Hughes, then magazine editor, bade farewell with a potted history of the *Motorist*, explaining that it had become the victim of inflation.

'In these days of high- and rising print and paper costs, it no longer makes economic sense to go on absorbing the costs of producing and distributing the magazine. Even a hefty increase in the 12½p cover price per copy would do little to offset our soaring costs. And the economic difficulties that plague us all make it virtually impossible to achieve more revenue from advertisements. [*Vauxhall*] *Motorist* is not alone among motoring magazines in feeling the pinch of severely restricted advertising budgets.

To some extent the charming old style of *Vauxhall Motorist* was dated. Motoring was becoming more mundane and car ownership less a mark of distinction. Cheap cars, like the Viva E at £1,399, including tax, were what mattered. Tales of roadside picnics and pleasant roadhouses did not fit with the modern and cost conscious world which was going faster everyday, with Britain fighting to keep up and seriously in debt. Unlike other car makers, Vauxhall pay packets depended more on overtime and falling sales were sometimes upsetting for morale, leading to the 1977 strike. However, the company was lucky not to be plagued by the bad industrial relations threatening to drive other manufacturers, and particularly British Leyland, to the wall. As Len Holden's study of Vauxhall and the Luton Economy remarked, Vauxhall had the best industrial relations with only three

Another young lady poses on this fine early Vauxhall Cavalier. The model was launched in 1976 and revised well into the 1990s, with the turbo and V6 models. The type was also modified to take account of increasing vehicle security demands as boy racers and professional thieves set their eyes on this desirable model (not the girl in the picture, of course!). Safety improvements in 1993 featured twin side impact bars and driver's air bag. (Vauxhall Motors)

The first series Astra, an image showing the dramatic contrast between this late twentieth-century Vauxhall and the old Prince Henry. The car had a tranverse engine and the latest compund crank rear suspension. A 1.6 litre diesel was available from June 1982, but the original engines were 1.2 litre pushrod and 1.3 OHC. Cars had advanced a long way in so few years. The car had much in common with the Opel Kadett as the two companies worked ever more closely together to rationalise costs and create more European orientated cars. (Vauxhall Motors)

The Mark 11 Astra appeared in 1984, continuing until 1992. It has been compared to a jelly mould style, but the cabriolet offered a bit more flair than the standard saloon pictured here in Penzance in 2003. (Robert Cook)

unions, compared to Ford who had twenty-one. The company had also gone out of its way to promote sports and social facilities, even creating its own drama group and ladies choir.

The 1970s were the years of glam rock and trashy pop songs lyrics like 'Viva I'm off to sunny Spain' and Luton Airport was made famous by Lorraine Chase. But the economic outlook grew increasingly dim, even though PM James Callaghan became renowned for his 'Crisis, what crisis' comment. The decade ended with firemen's and refuse workers' strikes, and apparently an economic Messiah in the form of Margaret Thatcher, backed up by the ideas of Sir Keith Joseph. For Vauxhall the outlook looked grim. Facing foreign and home competition, the opportunities of EEC membership had yet to be revealed. Vehicle sales were down to 230,420 in 1979 and new investment was called for to get the company back where it belonged.

The Firenza ceased production in 1975 and the HC Viva in 1979. The Chevette crossed the decade threshold, continuing in production until 1984. A reliable, if not exciting car, it sold a total of 415,608 from introduction in 1975 while the now highly collectable 2300 HS/R rally version sold 450. The 1976 version of the Cavalier continued until 1981 and on into the 1990s through complete redesigns. Old treasures like the VX 4/90 series, Ventoras and Magnums, however, ended with the 1970s, with the workforce reduced to 33,000.

The 2 millionth car rolls of the Ellesmere Port production line in August 1990. (Vauxhall Motors)

General Motors invested heavily during the 1980s, producing the front-wheel-drive Astra and boosting the Cavalier range to fifteen models, with dealers of Britain driving 700 vehicles around Britain in 1981. Sales across the range reached 250,000 over the next two years. The Astra was styled for the age, being boxy and functional and available as 4-door saloon, 5-door hatchback, convertible and four-door estate.

Frank Ford recalled that toward the end of his career, in the 1980s, he went on to forward planning as to how models would be designed and timing of their introduction.

'There was a ten year programme which was supposed to be sacrosanct but it got changed every month. The writing was on the wall that engineering was going to move to Opel in Germany. My last few years were interesting with frequent visits to Germany to keep the Vauxhall flag flying. They were known as the Product Policy Sub Committee and were filtering meetings for the product policy committee for the big boys; the directors, once a month. I enjoyed visiting Opel, they were interested in getting the job done.'

Like the 1980s Cavaliers and Astra, Vauxhall's Viceroy was an outcome of the Opel link, being a luxury version of Opel's Commodore on a 105in wheelbase, with MacPherson front springing, live axle rear end, disc/drum servo brakes, an automatic option and central locking. The model was short lived, from 1981-82,

Military contracts had always been important to Bedford's growth and this picture shows one of their more unusual contributions, one of eleven riot control vehicles built on a TM chassis. It is pictured here at the Bedford gathering in August 2003. (Robert Cook)

replaced by the top of the range Senator CD. Good value at the time, a 3 litre engine took it easily to 125mph. The MKII version from 1987 made Vauxhall popular with police forces who had deserted the marque for Fords and Volvos during the 1970s. The new model was extremely luxurious and with a 24-valve, 3 litre engine, could match the performance of most getaway cars and miscreant motorists with a 140mph top speed.

Cavalier sales exceeded 1 million by July 1988, justifying the £122 million invested in the type. A four-wheel-drive variant was even available. More investment followed at Ellesmere Port, adding £56.3 million to the £85 million spent over the preceding four years. Evidence that all had been good judgement came with a net trading profit of £152 million at the end of 1988. Vauxhall was also ahead of competitors in offering owners of post-1985 vehicles the chance to convert to them to lead-free running, free of charge. The decade ended with more record profits, with Vauxhall car registrations reaching an all time high of 349,901.

Maragret Thatcher reluctantly departed from government following the poll tax debacle, economic and EEC policy disputes. By this time, her government had overseen the crisis at state-owned British Leyland, where the truck division had been targeted by DAF. The outcome would see DAF benefiting from future army contracts and make the continuation of the Bedford marque unattractive to GM, in a world already oversupplied with truck and bus chassis. The stage was set

One of the latest Vauxhall Corsa saloons, continuing BSM's long traditon of using Vauxhall cars.
(Robert Cook)

for Scandinavian domination of these markets. Ironically Leyland had once been a major exporter to Scandinavia, but Britain had set its faith in an IT and service-based future. Bedford became AWD for a short while, but the old Dunstable manufacturing base now includes a supermarket and little scope for old skills.

An overheating boom in 1988-90 increased inflation, but when the credit boom was checked, a recession followed. General Motors wisely saw Vauxhall's future more assured through a continuing process of integration with General Motors Europe (GME) as they were already supplying many body panels and all of GME's ECOTEC V6 engines. Once again Vauxhall were showing others how to make an export drive, receiving the Queen's Award for Export achievement in 1992, even though demand for cars in Europe had fallen by 21 per cent in that year. Having a 17.09 per cent market share, Vauxhall were the highest-earning British volume car maker, declaring £185.1 million profit.

The small Vauxhall Nova ceased production in 1993 when the very popular Corsa name first appeared. The first model retained the torsion beam rear end and McPherson strutts of the old Nova, but wheels were placed at each corner, creating Mini-style glamour. The car also offered 16-valve performance and economy.

The ECOTEC V6 engine plant at Ellesmere Port opened in Autumn 1992. First fitted to the Calibra, ECOTEC stood for Emissions, Consumption, Optimisation

 **VAUXHALL**   Vauxhall - Ready For August

A range of new models for August 1993. (Vauxhall Motors)

Technology and engines featured four valves per cylinder, doubling the rate of
fuel and exhaust gas handling and managed by electronic ignition. The results
minimised fuel consumption and therefore pollution. Production was being
increasingly stepped up at Ellesmere Port, which, looking at the cost and transport
problems associated with the congested south-east of England and job shortages
around Liverpool, made abstract sense, However, there would be significant impact
if manufacturing jobs were ever to be seriously in doubt around Luton.

Significantly, what had been a trendy 1960s engineering and styling centre in
Osborne Road, Luton, was revamped into something rather different in the 1990s.
It became known as Griffin House, Vauxhall HQ. The new style, smoked glass
exterior and impressive waterfalls and giant plants of the reception area, make
a perfect background for displaying some of the company's latest models. Soon,
however, none of them would be built in Luton, where the main story had begun
back in 1905.

For the time being there were no doubts about the Luton plant, which also
made vans under the Vauxhall badge. The Omega replaced the Carlton and
Senator ranges in 1994, raising production to higher safety and security levels as
well as luxury and the Monterey moved the company into the four-wheel-drive
market which had long been a Land Rover monopoly. In the same year, Vauxhall
earned ISO 900 approval for its total manufacturing operations, underlining its
high quality performance. As part of this, Luton's future seemed assured by £136

Top of the range Vauxhalls make ideal police cars, as we can see with this Omega following Milton Keynes Carnival parade in July 2001. (Robert Cook)

This 1990 Bedford badged van of Japanese origin is an early example of the IBC link up. Photographed in Morab Road, Penzance, it carries a thought provoking message, due to a little interference from a passer by no doubt. (Robert Cook)

Gary Sowerby's ' round the world' Fronterra. The design is contrasts with Land Rover's more staid image. (Vauxhall Motors)

million investment in modernisation of the body, trim and final assembly plants. This included over 400 robotic welding and handling systems that would be needed for the forthcoming Vectra as the Cavalier was phased out – the last and 1,687,368th rolling of the line on 21 July 1995. Vauxhall looked forward with great optimism, a mood justified by £3.6 million in turnover and exports of 92,500 vehicles.

The firm's ninetieth anniversary was celebrated the following year with the Vectra's launch at the National Motor Show. This type marked Vauxhall's return to the estate car market as one of the Vectra options. Vauxhall continued to match new emissions regulations which were effective from 1997, with 80 per cent of their range up to specification by April 1996.

Vans were still an attractive market, but their lineage with a long line of Bedfords was sadly hidden and new ideas were the result of European collaboration and from links with Isuzu, leading to the sub-division Isuzu Bedford Commercials (IBC) which was formed in 1987 and operating from the old AA block. Vauxhall, IBC, General Motors and Renault signed an agreement in December 1996 to design and construct a new van. Investment of £180 million made 900 more jobs and saw the development of the new medium van range.

The plant also housed production of the second wave of Vauxhall four-wheel-drives, the Frontera – introduced in 1991. Such contributions to the motoring world have earned them nicknames like Kensington tractors owing to their

None the less, Fronterras are a very popular town and city vehicle as this scene from Edinburgh's North Bridge attests, in May 2000. (Robert Cook)

popularity with affluent town mothers taking their offspring to school and adding to traffic congestion, They do have more practical possibilities, particularly in countries short of made-up roads and proved successful in endurance events. One was driven around the world in twenty-one days, two hours and fourteen minutes, covering 18,344 miles in 1997. Driving team leader Garry Sowerby described the event as 'a 'pure driving record... one that would be hard to beat.' The model's new Sport RS version appeared in 1998, resulting from a £100 million investment programme, followed by a new Vectra in 1999.

The Vectra offered around 3,000 improvements, including chassis and steering. Safety was enhanced to include an active headrest system, designed to pivot on impact, reducing neck load by 50 per cent. A GSi Vectra with highly tuned 2½ litre V6 engine made an impact on release in July 1999, following on the tail of revised version of Vauxhall's MPV Zafira. The Zafira was built in GM's Bochum plant, yet another sign of the globalisation of car-making, a necessity in a fiercely competitive world. This innovative model made good use of TV advertising, and six months after launch the 100,000th had been built. It was voted best MPV by *What Car* and *Diesel Car* magazines in their 2000 car awards.

Vauxhall opened a new £5 million engineering centre at Millbrook, Bedfordshire in May 2000. Though close to Vauxhall's origins it was very much an international affair, providing global research and sharing developments with Opel. Similarly, the £2.6 million Customer Care Centre, which opened in April 2001, was multi-lingual and designed to cater for customers from all over Europe.

Japan's motor industry learned from assembling British kits and improving them. While the British industry was mired in nineteenth-century antagonisms, Japan was profiting from a more paternalist outlook and getting on with the job. Vauxhall, as we have seen, also valued its labour force, seeking to treat them well but unable to escape a national environment and poor examples from elsewhere which were not always conducive to enterprise. All Europe needed to take stock of a changing market place and emerging world economy. Joint agreements in the absence of outright takeovers were a necessity. When Luton workers heard, in the run up to Christmas 2000, that Vectra production would cease in March 2002, there was inevitable outrage.

On 13 December 2000, *The Times* leader commented:

'The entire car industry is faced with the problem of over-capacity, a dilema that is reinforced by the knowledge that labour costs outside Western Europe are lower than within it. If this were likely to be but a short-term challenge then Vauxhall could legitimately be denounced as behaving in an unreasonable manner. In truth, though, the medium outlook is not one that will encourage optimism among senior executives. If there is over capacity when the main European markets are experiencing (admittedly variable) economic growth, then the probable pattern in recession when demand would inevitably fall is very disturbing. The tricks by which additional profits could be squeezed out of European sales are also, rightly being eliminated.'

Managing director Nick Reilly understood the decision to cease Vectra production and close down Luton, with the exception of IBC. He was in a position to understand the necessity. Luton was after all a cramped location, making forty-two cars per man compared to nearer seventy in Europe. For Vauxhall's Luton workers it was about a job for life and paying for the coming and later Christmases. The announcement was painfully timed. As one told me:

'I joined the protest march. It was bitterly cold by the time we got to George Stereo. About 10,000 marched. Employees came over from Rover who feared for their own jobs. I was angry. We were technical staff, our jobs were safe. I believed they had made a wrong decision for the employees. Now one of the factories has gone, I think everything else will go. They can't shut IBC because the Spanish plant can't meet demand. Where's the new industry to take its place. Everyone got on at Luton's plant. Multi-cultures worked well. They are far more militant at Ellesmere Port.'

CHAPTER THIRTEEN

BOLD AND INNOVATIVE

Key facts were that GM Europe lost $181 million, in the last quarter of 2002 as well as having GM's global dominance threatened by a Japanese rival. For all the efforts, including Bill Murray from the TGWU, Luton production ceased on schedule. To cope with the fall out, *The Times* suggested that the DTI needed to combine meaningful assistance with economic realism. It carried the advice:

> 'Turbulence in the motoring world is unavoidable, but it is not the case that all manufacturing, even in this industry, is leaving Britain... the numbers of people employed in automobile manufacture is bound to fall here, those in the viable sectors of this industry may well be more secure in their employment. The best policies that this or any government can pursue are those that assist the long term prospects of precisely these individuals.'

This did not discourage many worker's view that it was easier to sack British workers than Europeans. Angry scenes happened as the final car came of the Luton line on 3 March 2002 and many were not placated by being given a commemorative book about the history of car-building on the site. Some lucky ones were going on to IBC next door, but in all 1,900 jobs were about to go.

Worse still, more manufacturing was leaving Britain. As observed by Len Holden in *Vauxhall and the Luton Economy*, Electrolux, Coulter Electronics, Laported and SKF all closed at the end of the 1990s. Luton's official unemployment rate was counted at a significant 4 per cent compared to the national average of 1.4 per cent, and was clearly disproportionately a male matter. Luton has also been voted the 'crappiest town' in a national pole, topping a list of others where traditional industry has departed. So called 'Mc jobs', from the likes of fast food outlets and part-time supermarket shelf-stacking jobs booms have been criticised as a feeble replacement for old skills which gave self respect to so many, particularly men.

Strenuous efforts are being made to promote new opportunities for Luton and to single the town out for special derision is not helpful. Nonetheless, there are serious issues to be faced. A rather steam-rollering scheme for the doubling of Milton Keynes will inevitably increase the morning outflow of commuters along the Watling Street and M1 to that area. Meanwhile, there is talk of revamping

A newly arrived Minaro at Vauxhall's Osborne Road vehicle park. (Robert Cook)

Luton and building more houses. Whether there will be much of a future for manufacturing in Luton, out of all this, remains to be seen.

New Vauxhall cars still roll in and out of Luton, on the backs of huge transporters. Such are the economics of car-making that Minaro models arrive, covered in waxed paper, all the way by ship from GM Australia. These powerful motors are certainly at home on a site which began life building vehicles for competition standard. One wonders what those pioneers imagined their enterprise would look like so many years on.

The sport tradition is, of course, alive and thriving. ECOTEC V6 power units proved the perfect mate for the VX220, a result of collaboration with Lotus and a chance to revive the VX badge which first appeared on a 1931 coupe and disappeared with the Victor range in 1978. The VX reached its apogee with the unveiling of the VX Lightning in 2003, becoming the centrepiece of the centenary celebrations, and featuring an all-aluminium ECOTEC 2.2 litre supercharged engine capable of 240bhp. Managing director Kevin Wale told *Vauxhall Mirror*:

'The VX Lightning says everything about where Vauxhall is heading. The car represents a return to our performance roots while we continue to be both bold and innovative in exterior and interior design. It is a classic roadster and represents the best of our past, and our future – a vehicle that is quintessentially British.'

As the advert shows, a Vauxhall dealer near Helston, Cornwall, offers a £2175 saving on a new Vauxhall Astra. (Robert Cook)

These sentiments were evocative of the 1930s and the 'all-British Bedford', which in a sense was still going strong with the production of the 100,000th Vivaro van which was handed over to the AA, an organisation that had grown alongside Vauxhall. It just seems a pity the van could not carry the Bedford badge so that the claim 'you see them everywhere' could live on.

There was more good news from VX Racing with Vauxhall about to defend its British Touring Car Championship crown in 2003. Meanwhile John Burton, Executive Director of General Motors Europe's Global Manufacturing Systems was leading Ellesmere Port's turnaround programme. John had experience dating from troubled times at British Leyland's now defunct Oxford plant and was particularly interested in attendance levels, the number of cars built right first time, unscheduled overtime and a shortfall in the total number of cars being built. The initiative was coming from high level. John felt that there was a need to look at additional training needed to improve skill levels. He told *Vauxhall Mirror*:

'Listening to the workforce may not have been a management strong point here in the past, but the Griffin turnaround team is determined to be receptive to the views and suggestions of employees.'

He explained:

'There is an awful lot of work to be done to turn the Ellesmere Plant around but it all comes down to individuals taking responsibility for their own contribution to the collective goal... I hope employees understand the degree of urgency associated with the turnaround programme...'

A Vauxhall Vectra on the M25 motorway near Heathrow, September 2004. British roads have not
kept pace with demand and public transport offers no discouragement because it is poorly funded,
inadequate, infrequent and inflexible. (Robert Cook)

The United States pioneered the human relations school of management, which
basically required management showing that they valued the humblest member of
the workforce, if for no better reason than if only one of them threw one spanner
in the works, they could foul it all up. John Burton had seen the worst at British
Leyland and where it had got that company. He was not going to fail at Ellesmere
and by 5 March 2004 the fifth generation of Astra was rolling off the production
line. BBC and ITV news teams were there to broadcast the excitement. The new
Astra went on sale in the UK on 1 May 2004, with the Ellesmere-built Opel
version on sale in Ireland two weeks earlier. Since its launch in 1980, nearly
2 million have been sold in the UK. GM chairman Richard Waggoner, unveiling
the new model, said the car gave the company 'a chance to move its image up
to the next level'. The 'nature of the styling and handling' showed that Vauxhall
was aiming for younger buyers. After touring the Ellesmere Plant, he praised the
teamwork at Ellesmere that had brought forward the start of production by almost
a month. He thanked union leaders for their support.

The car industry worldwide still faces an uncertain future. An economist report
of 23 February 2002, argued:

'As the industry's relics are razed, the shape of car manufacturing will change radically. The
ultimate pattern, according to industry seers such as J. Feron of Price WaterhouseCoopers, is
that today's metal bashers will disappear. In their place will be vehicle brand owners (VBOs).

MPV's like this Penzance Vauxhall taxi are very currently fashionable and a great boon to the motor industry. (Robert Cook)

They will do only the core tasks of designing, engineering and marketing vehicles. Everything else, including even final assembly, may be done by the parts suppliers. This already happens with niche cars, such as the Porsche Boxster. The task of American manufacturers is to bring their relations with suppliers into line with Japan's. Ten years ago, the big three manufactures in Detroit turned aggressively on their suppliers as they sought to recover from heavy losses. The charge was led by Jose Ignacio Lopez, head of purchasing at GM, but the others soon followed, demanding more price cuts.

Of course this is not a tale of wicked bullies exploiting defenceless suppliers. It is a difficult situation in an industry of over-capacity. As the *Economist* went on to explain, pressures for change have been building up in the industry. The longer poor returns continue, the harder car companies and parts suppliers struggle to raise affordable capital. High sales against heavy discounts are not sustainable and the Japanese are proving fierce competitors in the SUV market – the Opel Astra's price was cut by £750 providing orders were placed before the mid-March 2004 launch, but a similar offer was not made for the Vauxhall version, for which customers had to pay between £10,995 and £17,645, depending on model choice.

In February 2004, *Vauxhall Mirror's* front page carried the headline 'Best of the Best Vans'. As the *Economist* report went on to point out, the industry's failures were masked in 2002 by an unexpected boom in profitable sales of mini vans and sports utility vehicles (SUVs). The *Mirror* report showed how valued this sector had become, as it always had been through Vauxhall's long link with Martin

These days style seems to be everything, not least in ladies' fashion. Always up to date, Vauxhall teamed up with rising fashion designer Giles Deacon, who studied at London's St Martin's College of Art before going to work for the Gucci Group, and transformed a Corsa into a fashion statement on wheels. Vauxhall's head of communications, Charlotte Dunkley, said, '*We love Giles sense of style and design ethic.*

'*Most people now have a car and we think that style conscious Brits want their car to reflect their tastes.*

'*Innovative design is at the heart of future cars to be launched by Vauxhall…*

'*Vauxhall is an established British Company and Giles is fast earning a reputation as a leading British designer… Giles is already working on a number of projects for us.*' (Robert Cook)

Walter's Dormobile company. In 2004, the report explained that 'the sales and marketing team from Vauxhall's Commercial Vehicles (CV) has been named the 'best of the best' in the GM Chairman's honours programme, following a record-breaking performance by Vauxhall in the UK vans market last year.

'The Luton based team is among an elite fifty around the world whose accomplishments are judged to have made 'significant contributions' towards GM's world business objectives.'

Life on the road, a subject well chronicled by *Vauxhall Motorist* and the Bedford magazines, has changed. Once there was a world of carefree roadside picnics and neat roadhouses with a welcoming Bedford Drivers Club plaque for the weary pre-war truckers, or lorry drivers as they were known then. Now the road is not so open and the roadhouses, though with lots of shiny buildings, are not so revered. British roads, if media reports and experience are anything to go by, are well overloaded. Everyone wants to be out there, commuting, leisure driving or shopping – why not when public transport is so bad? An SMMT report, from October 2003, revealed that falling prices and cheap finance were fuelling a £5.5

Some people just like it the way things used to be, like the man way back in 1930 who wondered why when Vauxhall had it so right that there had to be a next years' model. They certainly don't make them like this 1968 CA Bedford van anymore. It was still doing a good job of work for Greenhands gardening services when this picture was taken in September 2004. (Robert Cook)

billion car buying boom, with that September's sales figures at 439,365. Rising property prices were supposed to a part of the feel-good factor encouraging purchasing, along with the new 53 number plate. Top of the list of the Top 10 selling models was the Vauxhall Corsa, at 18,283. The Astra was fifth at 14,130.

Meanwhile, the Government stood accused of breaking its own traffic congestion targets and pollution when it was revealed that ministers and officials were being ferried around in a record number of chauffeur-driven cars. A *Guardian* report from 18 December 2002 observed that the average engine size of their cars had also increased, despite official policy to encourage private company car drivers to use smaller, cleaner and more efficient cars. The Government's car fleet had grown by twenty, to 207, over the previous two years.

Transport studies also suggest that ever-increasing traffic means that by 2010 drivers will spend an extra thirty-five hours a year in their cars. Friends of the Earth said their predictions were an indication of how ministers failed to approach the problem of congestion or provide an alternative to the car by sorting out the rail network. Comments came in the light of Minister Alastair Darling's admission that he was abandoning another key pledge made in his Ten Year Plan for Transport. Minister Darling warned that traffic congestion was likely to rise by between 11 per cent and 20 per cent by 2010. Although demand for railways has slightly increased, train punctuality has fallen from 87 per cent before the Hatfield

A second hand Astra may top the wish list for used cars, but it will be a long time before Mick Walters, of Swanbourne Station, will wish to part with this well kept Astra 5 door. (Robert Cook)

crash to 79 per cent even though demand has surged. Bus use increases, but way behind the growth in car usage. There is considerable reluctance to promote and fund alternatives to the motor car, schemes like the Portsmouth tram and light railway proposals have encountered insurmountable obstacles and opposition.

The new town of Milton Keynes is set to double in size over the next thirty years but hopes to increase public transport use from 4 per cent to 16 per cent over the period have been virtually abandoned. Milton Keynes was designed for the car and expansion panel leader Alan Richardson reported that there was little hope of achieving a modal shift. Even though they expect Vehicle to Carriageway ratios of 106 per cent, they see make no recommendations for urgent transport improvements. In a settlement which struggles to maintain nearly 1,000 miles of grid roads, Cabinet Member Graham Mabbutt says it would be too much to gamble on investment in a tramway.

So the future of the car must be measured against this uncertain background. The modern motor car may seem a far cry from the first Vauxhalls, they are certainly safer as falling casualty rates attest, but most still need petrol or diesel. To sudden a shift to other technologies or forms of transport would make many skills redundant. A company like Vauxhall, backed by wealthy parents GMC, must keep an eye on world events and look for trends. Better still, they must even be anticipate them. However, it will prove hard to wean some of us off our big internal combustion cars. Thus it is not surprising that Quentin Wilson exhorted the virtues of GM's 5.7 litre V8 Insignia. Writing in the *Sunday Mirror* on

Sadly, though, this is the fate of most vehicles, though this sixties Victor FB stands some chance of resurrection, pictured here in the back yard of West Country Classic Restorers near Prussia Cove, Cornwall. Cars are about style, comfort and fashion statements, especially as it's increasingly hard to use them to get from A to B. So we will still want new models for years to come. But there are huge question marks about the future of transport in Britain and the world. (Robert Cook)

9 November 2003, he proclaimed: 'Of all the concept cars in all the world, this one really should be built. GM's Insignia is quite simply the best looking Vauxhall ever and the perfect opportunity to change the Griffin's image for good.'

Whether or not that is wise advice for Vauxhall remains to be seen in these troubled times, though clearly the Insignia would find a market as a niche car, built by the kind of small scale, subcontracting methods advocated by the *Economist*. A more broad-based future must reside in the outcome of Vauxhall projects like the hydrogen-powered Zafira which was previewed at the Geneva International Motor Show. The Zafira's fuel cell takes the car up to 87mph, with a range of around 250 miles. The electric engine emits only water vapour. Research is being carried out at Vauxhall/GM Global Alternative Propulsion Centre, which has bases in Germany and the US. In the age of computer design and mass communications, it is hard to imagine what will actually come to pass in the world of transport, but it is hard to imagine a motoring world without Vauxhall. The next 100 years should be at least as very interesting as the past 100.

Opposite bottom: Old Vauxhalls and Bedfords were so well engineered that many are still running worldwide. This left-hand drive ex-military tanker is seen here in service at Lands End Airport in August 2005. (Robert Cook/Isles of Scilly Steamship Co.)

Above: Chairman and managing director of Vauxhall Motors, Kevin E. Wale. Born in Melbourne Australia in 1954, Mr Wale is also vice president of General Motors. A graduate of Melbourne University, he joined Holdens in 1975, after working in various offices of the Finance department, he moved to GM Corporate Finance Department in New York, from 1983-5 and then back to Holdens in Australia, ultimately becoming director of sales, marketing and after sales until 1998. He was then appointed executive in Charge of Operations for GM Asia Pacific (Pte) Ltd in September 1998, based in Singapore. In August 2001, he moved to become MD of Vauxhall and vice president of GM Europe (GME) and member of the European Strategy Board in November 2002. Chairmanship of Vauxhall Europe followed in October 2004 and added responsibilities for GME's Commercial vehicles. October saw the the announcement of more Vauxhall redundancies at Ellesmere and in GM Europe.

Kevin Whale has now moved on within the organisation. (Vauxhall Motors)

SOMETHING ELSE

The Vauxhall Owners' Club is dedicated to promoting the restoration and use of old Vauxhalls, but the club wouldn't count this fine old Cresta PA because it was one of the first not to have bonnet flutes. It is owned by Dennis Sikoldi and still in regular service.

Keith Oakley and his 1972 Vauxhall Victor, purchased in 1972 from Shaw & Kilburn in Ayelsbury and sold on to two neighbours, including the present owner. It has less than 58,000 miles on the clock. Keith's only complaint is that its old fashioned bulb lights don't compare with halogen, so he can't speed at night. He calls the car, affectionately, 'Mr Meldrew'. (Robert Cook)

Dave Allen's custom Corsa Sport. Retired Vauxhall engineer and Vauxhall Owners' Club secretary Barry Harvey said he has seen the company move away from the dark days when the cars were reliable but unexciting – even being known as 'rust buckets'! (Robert Cook)

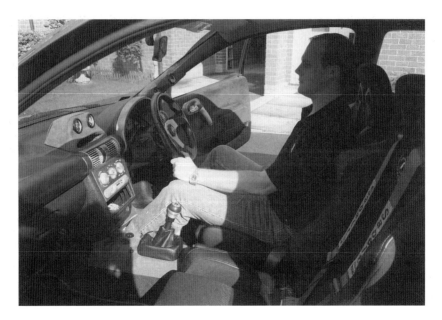

Interior of Dave Allen's Corsa. The car's 1398cc four-cylinder sixteen-valve engine delivers 100.2bhp and a maximum speed of 125mph. Barry Harvey said the company has gained a reputation for sports models in recent years, largely due to the influence of various managing directors. (Robert Cook)

BERNIE PARDUE

Bernie says he has always chosen Vauxhalls. He was one of the first into the company's Ellesmere Port plant in 1964. He said:

'I was a bus driver in Birkenhead and took a coach load of schoolchildren to a factory tour when it first opened. There was a fellow I'd worked with on the buses. He said, I should get a job there, so I did, in 1964. I think they expected us all to come to work on bikes, because they had built a big bike shed, and few car parking spaces.

'I worked on the line fitting glass visors, and side windows. It was hard work, but I wasn't going to let it beat me. I stuck at it. They were building cars with bodies painted in Luton. The bodies came up on a train - known as ' the rainbow express' because of all the colours- from Luton everyday.

'I was promoted to management group foreman as foreman supervisor, and went on training courses. I was responsible for all water sealing on the HC Viva, then on to quality control in the body, paint and press shop.

'We had a very good hard core of labour at Ellesmere Port. There was about 10 per cent from Liverpool, but we weren't going to let them push us around. I remember the plant manager, introducing himself saying his name was Derek Bell, short pants and no hair,

Bernie Pardue with his Vauxhall Zafira. (Robert Cook)

"you'll recognise me", he said. One Liverpudlian was walking out to the gate when Derek drove slowly through the crowd going off shift. This fellow opened Derek's car door and said "drop me at the gate mate." And Derek said "all right, hop in". Respect for Mr Bell dropped through the floor. They would have respected him a lot more if he'd told the worker where to go.

'Scousers have a reputation for trying it on, and Luton management were scared by it. There had been an idea that Vauxhall were training sheep, but there were a lot of skilled men, trained in aircraft and shipbuilding. We made body panels for the Opel Cadet, and sent them out to Bochum. The Germans resented that and found fault, but they didn't like it when we rejected their panels for the Viva.

'There was a lot of rivalry with Luton as well. They said we'd close within six years, but it was their place that went. And we nearly did close during the three-day week in 1974. We only had enough material for a couple of hundred Chevettes.

'We had some strong union men and managment were wary. Tony Woodley, who became Gen Sec of the TGWU, was there and I worked with his old man, George. There was also a lot of humour. I remember the management dinner when Tony Potter had to ask who had stolen the candelabra.

'When John deLorean visited with other GMC top brass, I had to organise his route through the plant. When I left the plant in 1978 to become a recruitment consultant, DeLorean became one of my clients and he remembered me. Now, John DeLorean was something else.'

INDEX

If you are interested in purchasing other books published by Tempus,
or in case you have difficulty finding any Tempus books in your local bookshop,
you can also place orders directly through our website

www.tempus-publishing.com